ENTRÉE TO JUDAISM
FOR FAMILIES

RUOTA DEL
FARAONE, PAGE 126

TINA WASSERMAN

Entrée to Judaism
for Families

Jewish Cooking **&** *Kitchen Conversations*
with Children

URJ PRESS

New York

For permission to reprint, please contact:
URJ Press
633 Third Avenue
New York, NY 10017-6778
212-650-4120
press@urj.org

LIBRARY OF CONGRESS CATALOGING-IN-PUBLICATION DATA IS AVAILABLE FOR THIS TITLE.

Book design by Judith Stagnitto Abbate / Abbate Design

Printed on acid-free paper
Copyright © 2014 by Tina Wasserman
Manufactured in Canada
10 9 8 7 6 5 4 3 2 1

To my children, Jonathan and Leslie, whose love and presence in my life has influenced me immeasurably and brought me great joy. Their sensitivity to others and ethical behavior exhibit the tenets of Judaism daily. I am confident that our family traditions and religious heritage will find a place in their lives and the lives of the next generation.

And to Frances *z"l*, aka "the Donut Fairy," who dedicated her life to her children, grandchildren, and Judaism. She instilled in her family a love of our traditions inside and outside the kitchen.

KALE, MANGO, AND
ALMOND SALAD, PAGE 58

CONTENTS

ACKNOWLEDGMENTS

Writing a book is like creating a new recipe. First you have to think about what ingredients you want to use, then you have to focus on the flavor balance and plate appeal. If the proportions are not right or the colors look too dull or clash on the plate, the cook will

not want to try the recipe and the diner won't want to eat it. Creating a cookbook requires that same attention to detail. The entries must be balanced in content and flavor to appeal to many readers. The pictures must intrigue the cook as well as reinforce what the dish will look like. And the stories and author's notes must follow the educational intent of the original theme. Although the author gets the credit, it is the many people supporting the project behind the scenes that need to be acknowledged.

First and foremost among those people is my publisher and editor, Michael Goldberg. Michael is young enough to be my son but wise beyond his years, which makes him my mentor and highly respected friend. His focus, support, patience, and unyielding confidence in me and the importance of my message—connecting and educating present and future

generations about their cultural and culinary inheritance—has allowed me to do what I love while giving back to my community. Stephen Becker, my marketing guru, patiently listens as I rattle off ideas and suggestions, sometimes jumping into the conversation before I can take a breath. Truth be told, it is sometimes difficult to assess who is more enthusiastic about my work, Stephen or me, and he is always thinking about disseminating the information I want to teach to all the cooks in the world, Jewish or not. He is the best cheerleader one could ask for.

When I compiled a spreadsheet of all the recipes in this book I noted the color of each food so that we could present it in the best way. You would be amazed as to the number of variations of brown that appear in cooking in general and Jewish cooking in particular. The glorious photographs in this book are the re-

sult of a great team. A simple "thank you" can never express the depth of my gratitude for the creativity, expertise, long hours, patience, and overall *menschlichkeit* (being a good person) exhibited by my photographer, Dave Carlin. With the help of Daniel, Sophie, and Chris Carbone, my prepared food was presented and shot in the most natural way to excite and entice. Ron Romaner used his considerable culinary skills to prepare some of the recipes when there weren't enough hours in my day to get everything cooked. I thank him for being a great friend and help. The food's neutral color palate was glorified by the beautiful art glass and accessories provided by Carlyn Galeries. Cindy Ray and Wendy Dunham have always been there for me to lend a hand, support my vision, and promote my books. They are the very best people and deserve my thanks. Bonnie Grossfeld, Debbie Postel, Elaine Stillman, and Liz Baron lent me terrific props for the pictures, but my real thanks go to them for their unconditional love and support. I also offer my gratitude to Jason Traub for editing the videos, to Debra Corman for again taking on the painstaking job of copyediting my stories and recipes, and to URJ Press staff members Fiorella de Lima, Jonathan Levine, Steve Brodsky, and Max Daniel.

I wanted to illustrate to the reader that I am truthful in my insistence that children can create the sophisticated recipes in this book, but there are no little children running around my house these days. Ben Krasner and Rebecca Hoffman are friends of the family, not professional models with a smudge of flour on their noses to make them look like they are having fun, but beautiful children who were thoroughly engrossed in chopping, grating, peeling, making monkey bread, and any other task they attempted. We all had a wonderful time working together and both children talked about their experience in my kitchen long after the shoot was over.

Carolyn Brienza, my former Mineola Junior High School student, submitted her Italian family's recipe for our end-of-year banquet forty-two years ago and I have kept that purple mimeographed sheet in my files ready to share one day with you. It was delicious then and it remains so today. My thanks also to Judy Zeidler for permission to adapt her recipe for turkey sausage from her book *Master Chefs Cook Kosher*. Thank you to my grandmother Gussie *z"l*, my mother Lucille *z"l*, and my mother-in-law Gladys *z"l* for creating culinary memories for me that I can share with all of you. Every time I make one of their recipes it keeps me connected to them and my past.

Of course, no amount of words could ever express my thanks to my children, Leslie, Jon, and Tanya, for their help and constant re-enforcement of my goals. But the biggest thanks goes to my best friend, my husband, Richard. He has helped me hone my writing skills, is the captain of my cheerleading squad, and deserves to share in every one of my successes.

INTRODUCTION

"Why didn't they ever teach us this when we were in Hebrew school?"

That was the first question asked of me after I had finished a program for my Sisterhood. I wasn't at the synagogue teaching Talmud or Torah or even the laws of kashrut. My presentation was held in the conference room of our local supermarket, and the discussion focused on the Jewish connection to many contemporary foods sold in that store. I had assembled eggplants, oranges, chocolate, olives, pomegranates, canned caponata, pita bread, and frozen fish and chips to illustrate my stories. Why were we connected to these foods? Where did they come from? How did our food choices become part of American Jewish culture? So many questions arose, and many were left unanswered during the program because we had overstayed our allotted time in the room!

Many questions lingered in my mind as well, which led me to write my column for *Reform Judaism* magazine for over ten years. Ev-

ery column had to be thoroughly researched. It was not sufficient to refer to the Sabbath Queen without substantiating the origin of that phrase. I uploaded an English translation of the Talmud onto my computer's desktop because I found that my queries often started or ended with that foundation of Jewish law. And all this research occurred long before I even began to investigate the recipes!

After my first book, *Entrée to Judaism*, was published—initiated by those first Sisterhood questions and instigated by the historical doors that were opened by my column—the book was premiered at the URJ Biennial in Toronto. Over 250 people came to hear my talk about the Spanish expulsion of the Jews in 1492 and its effect on world cuisine. The attendees thought that's why they came to the session, but I had a hunch that there was a different outcome in store for them and I was proven correct.

I schlepped two gallons of homemade chicken soup through customs for my talk. I had no intention of serving it to anyone! I put the simmering, golden soup in a large electric pot and placed it by the entrance to the meeting room. Everyone had to pass by the aroma of the chicken soup wafting through the air; I was setting the tone for the talk. Our olfactory senses are the most direct link to memory. Chicken soup is not just a wonderful aroma. It is the smell of the house getting ready for seder. It is the scent that wafts through the hall when you get off the elevator in your grandmother's apartment building. It is the memories of Friday nights around the Shabbat table either lingering with family and friends or eating fast to make it to services on time. It is much, much more than soup.

I enthusiastically sped through the talk, not realizing that I had left open a substantial part of the time allotment. What would happen if no one asked questions? That was not a problem. Hands rose immediately. One question led to an other. "How do I make my grandmother's goulash?" "My bubbe made hamantaschen with yeast dough; do you know how to make it?" "Do I really need to add a parsnip to my chicken soup?" "My mother has none of my grandmother's recipes; can you help me remember the name of the little spirals of filled dough? She came from Bulgaria." Over and over again I was bombarded with these questions. Did the people just need a good recipe or was it so much more?

Jews are often referred to as the people of the book, but I've come to realize that we're really the people of the cookbook! Our recipes represent who we are, where we came from, and where we live now. Our food choices are dictated by our culture and heritage. Did you ever wonder why the standard nut in *charoset* is walnuts? Why kreplach is often served in soup for Yom Kippur or why prune filling for hamantaschen is traditional? I constantly ask these questions about traditional dishes. The answers tell the stories of Jewish communities from around the world and across the centuries. Walnuts were the nut that was prevalent in Northern and Eastern Europe (a majority of Jewish immigrants to North America came from this region). Kreplach had its basis in a

medieval tradition of placing one's wish for the New Year in an amulet of dough and sealing it, hoping our lives would be "sealed" in the Book of Life for the coming year. And the tradition of using prune filling in hamantaschen was initiated to celebrate the acquittal of a prune jam merchant who was accused of poisoning a magistrate in Bohemia in the mid-eighteenth century.

All Jewish food, regardless of its regional world origin, is based on the laws of kashrut and the laws of Shabbat. You may not be *shomeir Shabbat* (refrain from work on the Sabbath) or follow the Jewish dietary laws restricting certain foods or preventing the co-mingling of meat and dairy products. However, I guarantee that on your seder table there is no shellfish or pork and no dish that contains both milk and meat. No recipe will ever be suggested for Passover, anywhere, that is contrary to these laws.

I have always encouraged my readers to contact me if they ever have a cooking question. One night, before Rosh HaShanah, I received an e-mail from a woman that said, "I am sorry to bother you but was wondering if you could help me? I grew up in Vienna. Every year my mother would make poppy seed strudel for Rosh HaShanah, and I haven't had it since I was seven years old and put on the *Kinder-*

transport." I was truly shaken. This woman was clearly in her seventies, and I didn't think she really wanted to learn how to make strudel for the first time—although I did create a recipe for her on the spot. What she really wanted was an experience to bring her closer to her mother again. That strudel's taste would bring her back to her youth before the Holocaust permanently separated the two of them.

Visiting and lecturing to Jewish communities around North America has shown me the desire and necessity to keep our culinary traditions alive. Teaching cooking to children and adults for over forty years has shown me the excitement and creativity that gets ignited when cooking becomes a history lesson filled with stories. These stories instigate conversations about our own family stories. They connect us to our ancestors and to the generations still to come. Most of all, cooking and creating with a child is an activity that will bring the participants closer together and create wonderful memories that will last a lifetime.

Cooking is a creative outlet for children. Look in any preschool classroom and you will find a play kitchen. Why? Because the kitchen is the hub of the household; nurturing takes place there, many of the best conversations happen there, and creativity abounds there. Years ago I offered Mom and Tots Cooking classes in my Manhattan apartment. A tiny two-line ad in the *New York Times* led to major stories and photo spreads in local newspapers, full enrollment in my classes, and even a segment on *Good Morning America*. I was teaching sophisticated adult recipes to the two- to four-year-olds and their moms—no banana snakes with raisin eyes for my students! Fresh pasta with sauce Mornay (aka macaroni and cheese), whole wheat pretzels, and classic chicken salad—as demonstrated on *GMA*—were some of the many nutritious foods taught in my school. The classes received significant attention because adults were looking for a creative learning experience for their children that also involved and engaged them in conversations about the food they were cooking and eating. Children explored the different tastes and textures of foods. Measuring taught them the daily importance of math in their lives long before tetrahedrons were introduced to them in geometry class. Hand cranking fresh pasta worked on their gross motor coordination. Chopping with an eight-inch chef's knife enhanced their motor skills while developing a sense of self-confidence and pride in their abilities.

Teaching children to cook at an early age provides a greater understanding of food preparation and often prevents them from becoming picky eaters. A child's exposure to *real* food—unprocessed, unadulterated, unsweetened foods—will promote better and more varied choices when eating in restaurants as well as during family meals. Since almost 30 percent of American meals are consumed outside of the home, this could have a great impact on a child's food experiences and overall health. When my son was nine years old, I gave him his own eight-inch, nonstick frying pan as one of his Chanukah presents so he could make his own scrambled eggs or grilled cheese sandwiches in his very own pan. You might think that he would have quizzically stared at us in disbelief. Instead, he clutched it to his chest and proclaimed that it was the best gift ever. Why? Because that gift was many gifts: it was the gift of independence, of self-esteem, of creativity, and of connection to the nurturing that took place in our kitchen. Even as a teenager, if he wanted to talk or just connect with me, he would hop up on the kitchen counter, dangle his legs, and sit. The kitchen is the heart of nurturing in any home.

Asking a child, "What do you want to cook?" is more effective if you give them choices. This book gives you that ability to engage and excite. Filled with delicious, international recipes and beautiful food photos, you will find what you need to complete a meal or create a snack that will provide unbridled enjoyment for both of you.

Create activities related to the recipes, to do perhaps while the recipe is cooking. *Zimsterne* cookies, traditional for *Havdalah*, could lead to creating your own *Havdalah* spice boxes from a small box or storage container filled with spices and decorated with crayon drawings or glued pieces of colorful paper. The activity of making bagels doesn't have to stop with a schmear of cream cheese. Why not cut up cucumbers, cherry tomatoes, olives, and sprouts and have the children make faces on their own "Mr. Bagel Heads"?

I hope you'll use this book in three ways. First, of course, enjoy some delicious recipes from Jewish communities and traditions from around the world; we all need to expand our repertoire of good foods. Second, enjoy interacting with children and sharing with them not only the excitement of creating in the kitchen but also the stories behind the recipes. Lastly, keep the kitchen conversation alive, the connections to our past relevant, and the culinary legacy deeply rooted so that the memories and stories will live on *l'dor vador*, from generation to generation.

Eat in good health!

List of Equipment

The kitchen is an educational lab. Learning names and tasks of cooking equipment not only expands a child's culinary knowledge but also facilitates finding the necessary equipment in the kitchen when you are ready to cook.

Below is a list of utensils and equipment that are found in most kitchens and used in the recipes in this book. I have also included some utensils that I find extremely useful in my own kitchen and that I feel are important to have when cooking with children.

Angled spatula, small
Apple corer/slicer
Baking dishes—8-inch square, 11 x 7-inch, 13 x 9-inch
Blender
Bundt pan
Casserole, covered—glass or metal
Casserole dish—3-quart oval
Colander
Cookie cutters
Cookie sheet
Cooling rack
Cutting board
Electric frying pan
Electric hand mixer
Electric stand mixer
Food mill
Food processor and workbowl with blades and disks

Food scoops/ice-cream scoops—1 tablespoon, 2 tablespoons, ¼ cup
Frying pan—10-inch
Grater
Jelly roll pan
Knives—chef's, paring, utility, table
Ladle
Loaf pan
Measuring cups—dry
Measuring cups—liquid
Measuring spoons
Microwave oven
Mini loaf pans
Mixing bowls—1 quart, 2 quarts, 3 quarts, 4 quarts
Nonstick frying pan—8-inch
Pancake skillet
Parchment paper
Pastry brush

Pizza cutter
Potato masher
Pots—1quart, 2 quarts, 3 quarts, 4 quarts
Pie plate
Pressure cooker
Roasting pan—13 x 9-inch or larger
Rolling pin
Rubber spatula
Small ingredient bowls—¼ cup, ½ cup, 1 cup, 2 cups
Soufflé dish
Soup pot—4–6 quarts
Spoons—large slotted and mixing spoons
Strainer—small, medium, and large
Vegetable peeler
Whisks—balloon, flat, and bar
Wooden spoons
Zester

List of Food Staples

Nothing could be more frustrating than coming into your kitchen prepared to cook a recipe and find that you can't make it because you are missing a key ingredient. What can you do? You can go to the supermarket, get the necessary item or items (invariably you forgot something else that was required), and return home to begin cooking, or you can decide to make something else.

This scenario becomes untenable when you are planning to cook with children. You have already lifted their expectations, and it is hard enough to contain their excitement while you are cooking so that the process is fun, is safe, and has a good outcome. You can't stop everything, pile the child into a car seat, and go off to shop!

Most recipes that are taste and task appropriate for a child can be made with basic ingredients found in your pantry, refrigerator, and freezer—that is, of course, if they are present at the time you want to cook!

The following list contains the foods that should be stocked in your kitchen at all times.

Personal taste will dictate your own personal "musts" that you need to have on hand. Some ingredients listed in this book might seem exotic to you, but I promise that once purchased, you will find many uses for them. I have included these ingredients in my "wish list." With the basics and some additional items from the wish list, you and your young sous-chef are ready to create a memorable and delicious experience.

Pantry

Applesauce—unsweetened
Apricot preserves
Baking chocolate—unsweetened
Baking powder
Baking soda
Beans, canned—black and garbanzo
Bread crumbs—unflavored
Bread—whole wheat, white, or challah
Chicken broth—canned and bouillon cubes
Chocolate chips

Cocoa—unsweetened
Cranberry sauce—jellied
Dried fruit—raisins, cranberries, dates
Extracts—vanilla and almond
Flour, all-purpose—bleached or unbleached
Grape jelly
Honey—preferably wildflower, but any kind will do
Ketchup
Mayonnaise—regular (not light)

Mustard—Dijon and ballpark (yellow)
Oatmeal—quick-cooking (not instant), old-fashioned, or regular
Oil—corn, canola, or vegetable oil and extra virgin olive oil
Pasta—spaghetti, macaroni, penne, or rotelli
Peanut butter—smooth or chunky
Pineapple, canned—crushed or rings
Salt—fine and kosher
Soy sauce—regular or low sodium
Spaghetti sauce

Spices and dried herbs—cinnamon,
cinnamon sticks, nutmeg, ginger,
cloves, allspice, coriander, paprika,
cumin, oregano, rosemary, thyme,
black peppercorns
Sugar—granulated, brown, and
confectioners'
Tomato paste
Tomato sauce
Tomatoes, canned—crushed in puree
Tuna fish in water
Vinegar—red wine or white
Worcestershire sauce

Refrigerator

American cheese
Apples
Baby spinach
Butter—unsalted
Carrots
Celery
Eggs—large size
Greek nonfat yogurt
Lemon and/or lime
Lettuce
Milk—skim, 2%, or whole
Onions and/or green onions
Orange juice
Oranges
Parmesan cheese
Potatoes—small red and/or Yukon
Gold

Sweet potatoes
Swiss or cheddar cheese
Tomatoes—large, Roma, or cherry

Freezer

Almonds—whole and slivered
Apple juice
Boneless breast of chicken, in 1-pound
packages
Broccoli
Cauliflower
Chopped spinach
Orange juice
Peas
Pecans
Vanilla ice cream
Walnuts

Wish List

Agave nectar—golden
Apple cider vinegar
Baharat—Middle Eastern sweet spice mix
Balsamic vinegar
Berries or fresh fruit in season
Bread flour
Chipotle or ancho chili powder
Corn syrup
Crisco sticks
Curry powder
Dried fruit—prunes, apricots, and dried
cherries

Dried mustard
Green chilies, canned—chopped
Kale
Molasses
Orange blossom water, bottled
Orange or lemon extract
Panko bread crumbs
Pasta shells—jumbo for stuffing
Picante sauce or salsa of your choice
Pine nuts
Pistachios—shelled, preferably unsalted
Pomegranate molasses
Poppy seeds
Rose water, bottled
Saffron
Sesame seeds
Smoked paprika—*pimentón de la Vera*
Sour cream
Tomato juice
Yeast—rapid rise or regular
Zatar—Israeli dried mixture with sesame
seeds

Part I

HOLIDAYS OR ANY DAY

APPLESAUCE,
PAGE 14

Fall

Ask children what the fall season means to them, and their answers will probably include going back to school, falling leaves, football, pumpkins, and colder weather. If the children are Jewish, there's a good chance they will add Rosh HaShanah and Sukkot to the list, because these two holidays stand out with their decorative symbols. Shofars, apples and honey, and white-draped Torahs are iconic for Rosh HaShanah, and decorated latticed structures draped with fruits and paper rings and golden leaves depict the huts, or sukkot, that the Jews temporarily lived in when they made their fall harvest pilgrimage to ancient Jerusalem.

From a culinary standpoint, fall means new crops from the farm. Apples, pears, pomegranates, pumpkins, squash, beets, cabbage, cranberries, and more find their way into the supermarkets, and most find their way onto our holiday tables. Rosh HaShanah requires the eating of a new fruit. In Israel the pomegranates are plentiful, and their numerous seeds (arils) are purported to equal the 613 mitzvot (commandments). Pumpkins and squash, with their golden color, have symbolized prosperity to Jews for millennia and find their way into culinary tradition.

Morsels of food wrapped in dough or cabbage are featured in this section because it is traditional to eat this type of preparation to symbolize our hopes to be "sealed" for a good life in the coming year.

Basic Chicken Soup

*C*hicken soup is made in kitchens around the world, but this clear soup with its little dots of liquid fat floating on top is so connected to Jewish cuisine that it is known as "Jewish penicillin" in America, probably because it makes you feel so good, especially when you are sick. Chicken soup was always served for Shabbat and at weddings, where the fat was allowed to pool on the top of the soup bowl to show the wealth of the bride's family.

One 4- to 5-pound roaster, cut into 8 pieces
5 quarts water or water to cover
1 parsnip, peeled and cut into thirds (optional)
1 large onion, peeled but left whole
1 turnip, peeled and cut into quarters
2 stalks celery with leaves, cut into thirds

3 or more carrots, peeled and sliced into 1-inch lengths
Fresh dill, 3 or more sprigs to taste
Fresh parsley, 2 sprigs or more if parsnip isn't being used
Salt and freshly ground pepper to taste
Kreplach (optional; see page 6)

1. Place chicken pieces in a 6-quart pot and cover with water.

2. Bring the water to a boil and simmer for 30 minutes, skimming the top of the liquid to remove all of the brown foam.

3. Add the remaining ingredients and cook over a low heat until the chicken is quite tender and the vegetables are soft, about 2–3 hours.

4. Remove the chicken with a slotted spoon. Discard the dill and parsley. Remove the vegetables to nibble on, and save the carrot for later use in the soup. Strain the soup so that it is nice and clear.

5. Place the soup in a clean pot, and add the carrots and cooked kreplach. Heat until nice and hot. Serve.

TINA'S TIDBITS

- *Cutting up the chicken to expose more of the inside of the meat to the water will produce a soup with a much richer flavor.*
- *Even if you don't keep kosher, use kosher chickens or organic chickens to make the soup. I once made this recipe in a friend's home using a well-known nonkosher chicken. The chicken shrank in half because it had been plumped with water, and the soup tasted like the chicken "ran" through it!*
- *An alternative to clear soup is to combine the vegetables with the broth in a blender until the mixture is opaque and creamy.*

Kitchen Conversations

Every family makes their chicken soup the way their families made it. Is your family's recipe similar to mine? Do you use dill or a different herb? Is your soup clear or creamy? There is no right or wrong way to make chicken soup, just different ways.

Chicken-Filled Kreplach

L *ittle soup dumplings called kreplach are served in hot chicken soup for Rosh HaShanah and the meal before the beginning of Yom Kippur. These meat-filled noodles date back over a thousand years ago, representing hopes that our fate would be "sealed" in the Book of Life for good health and prosperity in the coming year.*

Traditionally kreplach are filled with beef or liver. After making a big pot of chicken soup one year, it dawned on me that a healthier version could be made using some of the delicious chicken cooked in the soup!

Wing and 1 thigh from the cooked
   soup chicken—about 1 cup of mixed
   chicken meat (see "Basic Chicken
   Soup," page 4)
1 teaspoon minced fresh dill
1 tablespoon rendered chicken fat or
   chicken fat from the soup

Kosher salt and freshly ground black
   pepper to taste
8 ounces of fresh pasta dough or
   wonton skins
1 egg mixed with 1 teaspoon of water

1. Carefully remove the chicken meat from the skin and bone on the cooked chicken pieces. Shred the meat with your fingers to make sure that there are no bones.

2. Finely chop the chicken meat, and combine it with the dill, chicken fat, and seasonings.

3. If using sheets of pasta, cut the dough into 2-inch squares.

4. Place a teaspoon of filling on each square.

5. Brush the top edges of the dough with a little of the egg-water wash.

6. Fold the dough in half on the diagonal to make a triangle. Pinch the edges together and press down with the back of your pinkies to make a seal.

7. Cook in boiling salted water for 10 minutes or until done. Drain well in a colander. Serve in the chicken soup or, alternatively, fry in a little oil.

YIELD: 18+ PIECES

Kitchen Conversations

● What are your wishes for the New Year? Talk about hopes and dreams with older children.

● Write a wish on a piece of paper. Seal it in an envelope or decorate some construction paper and staple or tape it closed. Find a special place in the house to hide it until next year to see if the wish came true.

TINA'S TIDBITS

• *Wonton skins will make the kreplach a little thinner than bubbe's!*
• *It is more difficult to separate the meat from the bones in a small wing. If working with a young child, substitute a small amount of breast meat and shred finely.*
• *Many supermarkets sell fresh pasta dough or fresh lasagna noodles that are the right width. However, thicker wonton skins are a good substitute.*
• *If you remember chewy kreplach and are using wonton skins, stack two or three wonton skins, brushing some egg wash between each layer before filling them.*
• *This recipe can be made in stages. Make the filling and refrigerate it for up to 24 hours. Fill the kreplach and boil another time. Cool the kreplach completely before freezing.*

Hungarian Cabbage Strudel

The round, light-green vegetable we call cabbage became popular in Germany about nine hundred years ago. Because it was very easy to grow in cold climates like Northern and Eastern Europe, it was very popular in Jewish cooking, especially in the poor communities of Eastern Europe. Cooked in every way possible, cabbage was often found in soup, stews, or even pickled (sauerkraut). For festivals, cabbage was "dressed up" and stuffed or used as a filling in pastries, an alternative to costly nuts, fruit, sugar, and spices. The combination of cabbage and caraway seeds in this strudel was a classic Hungarian preparation.

Cabbage was very popular in Ashkenazic communities during all the Jewish fall festivals: sealed in strudel for Rosh HaShanah, as we hope to be sealed in the Book of Life for the coming year; served during Sukkot as a fall harvest food; and, according to culinary historian Gil Marks, served during Simchat Torah because the Hebrew word for cabbage, k'ruv, sounds like the word for the cherubim on the top of the Ark that held the tablets of the Ten Commandments.

---

1 pound cabbage (half of a medium head)	Salt and freshly ground pepper to taste
½ tablespoon salt	1 teaspoon caraway seeds
1½ sticks unsalted butter, divided	3 tablespoons dried bread crumbs
	8 sheets of phyllo dough

---

1. Cut the cabbage in half lengthwise, and then thinly slice it into shreds. Toss in a 4-quart bowl with the salt. Set aside for 15–30 minutes.

2. Using strong paper towels or a clean cloth towel, squeeze the water out of the cabbage and pat it dry.

3. Heat a 10-inch frying pan over high heat for 20 seconds. Add 4 tablespoons of butter to the pan. Melt the butter but do not let it brown.

4. Add the cabbage and sauté over medium heat for 10–15 minutes until the cabbage is soft and slightly browned. Do not burn.

5. Season to taste with salt, pepper, and caraway seeds. Place contents in a bowl to cool.

6. Melt the remaining butter in the microwave or in a 1-quart saucepan on the stove. Do not burn. Set aside.

7. Remove 4 sheets of phyllo dough. Keep the remaining sheets folded and covered by a sheet of plastic wrap, which is then covered by a damp paper towel.

8. Spread out a thin dishtowel or a sheet of waxed paper or parchment paper that is as long as the dough. Place 1 sheet of phyllo on the towel or paper, and brush it liberally with some of the melted butter.

9. Place another sheet of dough on top of the first, and brush with melted butter. Repeat with the remaining 2 sheets.

10. Lightly sprinkle half the bread crumbs over the last sheet, and then place half of the cabbage in a 2-inch-thick strip parallel to the long edge of the dough. Leave 1 inch of dough uncovered on each side so the cabbage can be sealed in tightly.

11. Using the towel or paper to help, fold the long side of the dough tightly over the

cabbage once. Brush the two short sides of the dough with some butter, and then fold them in about 1 inch on each side to cover the cabbage. Slowly lift the towel up to help you tightly fold the remaining dough into a roll. Place the finished roll, seam side down, on a parchment-lined, low-sided cookie sheet.

12. Repeat the process with the other half of the dough and the filling.

13. Preheat the oven to 375°F. Brush the tops of the rolls with melted butter, and using a sharp knife, lightly cut on the diagonal through a few layers of dough every 2 inches.

14. Bake the strudels in the center of the oven for 25 minutes or until golden brown. Cut through slash marks and serve.

Kitchen Conversations

● Did you know that broccoli and cauliflower are in the same family as cabbage? What do they have in common? Do you like one of these vegetables but not the others? Why?

● Does your family have special recipes that use cabbage? Were they served at special holidays or when the family celebrated together?

TINA'S TIDBITS

• *This recipe is more appropriate for children over the age of nine because slicing the cabbage, sautéing at the stove, and quick handling of the phyllo require more maturity.*
• *Younger children can create the strudel if you use packaged cole slaw (without carrots) and they are tall enough to work safely at the stove.*

Quesadillas

The first Jews of Mexico arrived with the Spanish conquistador Hernando Cortes in 1521. These Jews were Conversos or crypto-Jews, so called because they were forced by the Spanish Inquisition to become Catholic and had to practice their Jewish faith in secret. It is estimated that by the middle of the 1600s there were more crypto-Jews than Spanish Catholic in Mexico City. Over time, most of these Conversos and their descendants became faithful Catholics, though many continued to light candles on Friday night and keep their milk and meat foods separate.

Most of the Jews in Mexico today are descendants of Jews who immigrated from Eastern Europe beginning in the mid-1800s, as well as Sephardic Jews who left the fallen Ottoman Empire in the wake of World War I and German and other European Jews who fled Nazi-occupied Europe in the 1930s.

Although not necessarily traditional for the Jewish New Year, quesadillas are another food that "seals" in its goodness just like we hope our fate is "sealed" for good in the coming year.

---

5 large flour tortillas

2–4 tablespoons vegetable oil

4 ounces grated Chihuahua cheese, mozzarella cheese, or cheddar cheese

Any leftover cooked vegetables, like mushrooms, onions, or broccoli (optional)

Salsa or sour cream for dipping (optional)

---

1. Spread out the tortillas on a cutting board, and divide the cheese evenly over the bottom half of each tortilla, leaving a ½-inch rim around the bottom. Top with vegetables, if desired.

2. Fold the tortillas in half; brush the tops with some of the oil.

3. Heat a large griddle or 10-inch nonstick frying pan over medium-high heat for 15 seconds. Place a few of the quesadillas, oiled side down, on the griddle. Brush the tops of the cooking quesadillas with some oil.

4. Cook until the bottom is golden. Using a large turner, flip the quesadilla over, and cook the other side until golden and crisp.Remove to the cutting board, and cook the remaining filled tortillas.

5. Using a chef's knife, cut each tortilla into thirds or fourths, and serve plain or with salsa and/or sour cream.

NOTE: Fresh or grilled vegetables can be added to the cheese before folding and frying for a more substantial filling.

- *To make **Southwestern quesadillas**, top the cheese with 1 tablespoon sautéed onion, two thin slices of fresh mango, and 1 or more teaspoons of canned chopped chilies before you fold the quesadillas.*
- *The light brushing of the oil on the tortilla makes the quesadilla crispy on the outside and soft on the inside. No other oil is necessary.*
- *Children of all ages can make this, but children under the age of five should have direct supervision and help turning the quesadilla.*
- *If young children (aged three to four) start to get fidgety or argumentative when near the stove, calmly but immediately take them away from the cooktop. This is not a reprimand but a perfect time to discuss safety and actions having consequences. The quesadillas can wait.*

Kitchen Conversations

- Where are the members of your Jewish community from? Do you know any Jewish people who are from Mexico, India, or Africa?

- Why do so many Jewish people live in North America? What brought them here?

- If you are making quesadillas near Rosh HaShanah, talk about what hopes you would like to seal for the coming year.

Three-Ingredient Brisket

shkenazic Jews in Europe, generally being poor, could afford only less-expensive, tough cuts of meat that required a long cooking time to tenderize. Often only small amounts of meat were cooked along with large amounts of beans and vegetables (as in cholent, a slow-cooking Shabbat lunch dish). As immigrants to North America became more prosperous, larger portions of meat were cooked at one time, but the favored cut of meat was still the brisket, which required slow cooking for flavor and tenderness.

As times changed so did cooking techniques. Preparation time was often shortened even if cooking time remained long.

The following recipe is easy and delicious and part of my family's holiday traditions. When my daughter Leslie was studying in Rome one fall semester and couldn't be home for Rosh HaShanah, she wanted to re-create this recipe to feel closer to home. After she received ten slices of meat from the kosher butcher, because he was not familiar with or did not understand what "brisket" was, I showed Leslie over Skype how to follow this recipe with the slices pushed together, and I demonstrated the butcher's fold from fifty-six hundred miles away. There was no clearer lesson for me about how important a role memories play in our culinary heritage.

4- to 6-pound brisket
1 envelope of dried onion soup mix
12-ounce jar of apricot preserves

1. Place a large piece of extra-wide heavy-duty foil shiny side up in a roasting pan.

2. Sprinkle half the contents of the onion soup envelope on the foil.

3. Spread ½ of the jar of apricot preserves over the soup mix.

4. Place the meat fat side up (if there is a fat side) in the pan over the preserves and dried soup mix.

5. Sprinkle the remaining soup mix over the meat, and dot with the remaining preserves, being careful that the spoon for the preserves never touches the meat.

6. Make a butcher's fold with the foil: bring the long sides of the foil together and make 3 or 4 folds to seal close to but not tight on the meat. At either end, flatten the foil, fold up 2 times, fold the points in like you would wrapping a present, and then fold across the end 2 more times to seal the end. Repeat on the other side.

7. Place in a 300°F oven and roast for 4 hours.

8. Carefully open a corner of the foil and pierce the meat with a fork. If the fork goes in easily, the meat is done. If not, seal the foil and return to the oven for another 30 minutes. When the meat is fully cooked, carefully open the foil, and pour the gravy into a container. Chill the meat in the foil in the refrigerator until it is cold. Freeze for later use, or slice the cold meat on a slight diagonal against the grain.

9. When ready to serve, skim the fat off the gravy, pour the gravy over the meat, place in a microwave-safe container and cover with plastic wrap, and microwave on high for 5–6 minutes or until heated through.

TINA'S TIDBITS

- *Because opening the foil after roasting can be dangerous when the meat is very hot and steam escapes, only an adult should attempt this task.*
- *When spooning ingredients like preserves onto meat, it is very important not to touch the spoon to the meat's surface and then place it in the jar again. Bacteria from the raw meat can grow in the remaining contents in the jar and make people sick.*
- *It is much easier to slice meat when it is cold or at room temperature. Fat is also easier to remove from cold gravy.*
- *Always cut meat on a diagonal against the grain and consider reheating in a microwave. This prevents the meat from drying out and toughening.*

Kitchen Conversations

- Does your family have a favorite brisket recipe? How was it cooked? Was it cooked on the top of the stove or in the oven? Did it have special ingredients that represented your heritage (for example, caraway seeds from Hungary, pickles from Poland, or gingersnaps from Germany)?

- Has the family recipe changed over the years because of new kitchen equipment?

- Can you create your own recipe with your favorite ingredients? Be creative—sometimes chocolate can be used with meat too!

Applesauce

The majority of Jewish immigrants who came to the United States in the last 150 years trace their roots to Germany and Eastern Europe. Apple trees grew all over this region, and Jewish cooks used apples in dishes to make them special for Shabbat, Jewish celebrations, and Jewish holidays. Harvested as one of the first fruits in early fall, when Rosh HaShanah occurred, apples were dipped in honey to symbolize a sweet and fruitful year ahead.

Since they stored well, apples were eaten all through the winter and were made into applesauce. This was the original topping for potato latkes in the early 1800s, when potatoes became popular and latkes were served, first in Germany and later in Eastern Europe and Russia, at meat meals for Chanukah. (Sorry, no sour cream!)

Cooking the apples with their peel (where the flavor cells are located) gives it a pretty pink color and provides a natural sweetness, which means you can use very little or no sweetener. This recipe should be in every home's repertoire. It doesn't get fresher than this, and it is so easy to make, especially if you have a food mill.

1 cup water (or enough to fill pot ½ inch)

2-inch cinnamon stick or ½ teaspoon ground cinnamon

4–6 Fuji, Gala, or other sweet red apples

¼ cup sugar (optional)

1. Using an apple corer/slicer, core the apples and cut into eighths.

2. Cover the bottom of a 3-quart saucepan with ½ inch water. Place the cinnamon stick or ground cinnamon and the apples in the water. Cover the pot and simmer for 15 minutes or until the apples are very tender.

3. Remove the cinnamon stick and strain the water from the pot into a bowl. Set aside.

4. Place the apples in the basket of a food mill. Place the food mill on top of a 2-quart bowl. Following the manufacturer's directions, use the medium disk and turn the handle to pass the apple through the disk, leaving the skins in the basket and the applesauce in the bowl below. If the mixture looks too thick, add some of the reserved liquid and cool. Mixture will thicken when cold.

5. If desired, add sugar to taste. Serve warm or chilled.

YIELD: 2-3 CUPS

Kitchen Conversations

● Try a Fuji or Gala apple, or some other apple you have never tasted. Then taste a Red Delicious apple. These apples have been modified to withstand shipping, to have a beautiful color, and to be reasonably priced. Do they taste the same as the other apples? Discuss why you think this could be.

● Look at the colors of the apples. Which ones would make the applesauce very pink? Which would make it yellow?

TINA'S TIDBITS

• *If you don't have a food mill, strain the apples in a colander and save the cooking liquid. Wait for the apples to cool, then use your hands and a spoon to scrape the apple pulp into a bowl. Mash the pulp with a fork, adding a little of the reserved juice if necessary.*

• *Using a cinnamon stick creates the sensation of sweetness on the tongue, even with little or no sugar added.*

Quick Honey Cake

When the Israelites followed Moses to the promised "land of milk and honey," the honey referred to was not from bees but from fruit. Date honey was the most common honey in biblical times. Honey has long been eaten in many dishes for Rosh HaShanah by Jews around the world. Honey-soaked balls of baked dough (teiglach, *Eastern Europe*), semolina cake soaked in honey syrup (tishpishti, *Turkey*), and the famous European honey cake (lekach, *Germany*) are all desserts served as a wish for a sweet New Year. Lekach is by far the most popular cake served in North America for Rosh HaShanah.

One summer I needed a honey cake for a recipe I was creating and did not want to make one from scratch just to tear it apart. I went to the store and no honey cakes could be found (though there would soon be many come Rosh HaShanah time). What to do? I combined a standard gingerbread cake mix with some main ingredients in honey cake—coffee and honey— and an easy, quick honey cake was born!

¾ cup warm coffee (or ¾ cup water with 1 teaspoon instant espresso)	14.5-ounce box gingerbread mix
¼ cup honey	Eggs, as needed in mix
	Oil or margarine as needed in mix

1. Microwave the coffee with the honey for 30 seconds on high. Stir to combine.

2. Preheat the oven according to package directions.

3. Prepare the cake following the package directions except substitute the warm coffee and honey for all of the liquid in the recipe. Use the appropriate amount of oil and eggs called for on the package.

4. Grease a 9 x 4-inch loaf pan. Pour the batter into the prepared pan, and bake according to the time on the package mix.

5. Cool completely and then serve or use in Apples and Honey Cake Bread Pudding with Butterscotch Sauce (*Entrée to Judaism*, page 444).

TINA'S TIDBITS

- *Using boxed mixes is a good way to let young chefs begin to learn how to cook on their own. Misreading instructions once will leave an indelible impression that will make them more cautious the next time they cook. Believe me, I still remember the error I made when I was ten and used ¼ cup* **plus** *1 tablespoon instead of ¼ cup* **minus** *1 tablespoon in a frosting recipe!*
- *In general, it is not a good idea to use mixes, as they contain way too many additives and sugar. However, if the cake or cookie is being used to create a specialty dessert, then opt for less prep time to accomplish your goals.*
- *Decaffeinated coffee may be substituted for the instant espresso.*

Kitchen Conversations

- Different flowers create different-tasting honeys. Alfalfa honey is totally different from wildflower honey, and that is different from thyme honey. The flavor of the honey depends on where the bees are getting their pollen. What kind do you like?

- Did you know that honey is sold like olive oil? Both can be sold either as a blend from many different regions or as one flavor coming from only one type of plant.

- Is there a store in your neighborhood that lets you sample different honeys before you buy one? Go and have a tasting "bee."

ROASTED BUTTERNUT SQUASH
WITH APPLES AND ONIONS, PAGE 28

Winter

Although winter officially starts in December, cold air and gray skies descend upon many of us around early to mid-November. Whereas serving canned tomato soup accompanied by a grilled cheese sandwich might have been iconic cold-weather comfort food in the 1950s and 1960s, today's children have been exposed to a wider taste palate and are more likely to try new flavors and combinations of food in one dish. Let the soups in this section act as a springboard to trying new recipes with new ingredients and seasonings. Children of all ages like to add ingredients to a large pot of simmering goodies, and soups offer many experiences that can be isolated from the entire recipe in case your little chef's attention cannot be sustained throughout the entire process. Reading a rendition of the folktale "Stone Soup" complements the preparation of soup and also teaches empathy, sharing, and cooperation.

Winter also welcomes Chanukah, and where would we be without our symbolic fried foods? However, there is no reason that fried foods have to be greasy or devoid of good nutrition. Potato-crusted fish and sweet potato and carrot latkes will be a welcome addition to your holiday entertaining regardless of the holiday that you are celebrating.

Quick and Easy Tomato Vegetable Soup

he tomato was first grown and eaten by the Aztecs in Central and South America. When the Spanish conquistador Hernando Cortes brought the fruit back to Europe in the early 1500s, people did not eat it, because they thought it was poisonous. The Italians did begin to eat this new fruit in the late 1500s, and soon the tomato's popularity in Southern Italy was evident by its use in many food preparations.

The recipe for gazpacho—a tomato and vegetable soup that is served cold—was created hundreds of years ago in the southern region of Spain called Andalusia. Before the expulsion in 1492, many Jews lived in this region. Perhaps a soup containing no meat or pork fat might just have been invented by someone Jewish. Maybe not, but certainly a hearty soup of vegetables with tomatoes has been a staple of cooks the world over for a long time. Probably the most famous tomato soup in this country is Campbell's Tomato Soup, which was created in 1897.

Next to Campbell's, this is the easiest and most nutritious soup around! Many supermarkets package containers of freshly chopped vegetables. This convenience food will save a great deal of time, especially important when working with young cooks. I have listed the weight as well as the volume of chopped vegetables that you will need. Just make sure that you have some onion in the mix.

1. Heat a 4- to 6-quart pot for 15 seconds. Add the oil, heat for another 10 seconds, and then add the onions.

2. Sauté onions for 2–3 minutes until soft and starting to get golden. Add the remaining vegetables and cook for 3 minutes.

3. Add the remaining ingredients. Cover and simmer for 40 minutes or until barley is tender.

4. Taste and adjust the seasonings. Add sugar if necessary.

YIELD: 8 OR MORE SERVINGS

---

2 tablespoons extra virgin olive oil

2 pounds (5–6 cups) assorted vegetables (onion, zucchini, summer squash, peppers, corn, and broccoli), chopped

46-ounce bottle tomato juice

1 cup water

¼ teaspoon cumin

1 teaspoon dried thyme

½ teaspoon oregano

1 bay leaf

2 tablespoons pearled barley

2 cloves garlic finely minced

Kosher salt and freshly ground pepper, to taste

1 tablespoon sugar or honey (optional)

Kitchen Conversations

● Adding different spices and ingredients can transport this soup from Spain to Israel or Morocco or India. The addition of large Israeli couscous and a Middle Eastern spice mixture known as *baharat* will make this soup more Israeli. A Sephardic version of this soup might contain chickpeas or rice, cilantro or mint, cinnamon, peppers, and some saffron. Lentils and some curry powder and a little coconut milk will transport you to India.

TINA'S TIDBITS

• *Care must be taken if a young child is sautéing the onions. Use a long-handled spoon, and make sure the child's hand stays above the rim of the pot.*

• *Sugar is not necessary, but Italian cooks often add a small amount if the tomatoes are slightly bitter.*

Krupnick (Vegetarian Mushroom Barley Soup)

How long have Jewish people been eating mushrooms? A long time! Mushrooms were mentioned in the Babylonian Talmud (N'darim 55B), and wild mushrooms were in such abundance in ancient Israel during the rainy season that discussions arose about putting a tax on them. In later generations, mushrooms were especially important to poor Ashkenazic Jews. They were easily found in the forests, and since spices were expensive, their flavor, especially when dried, was a boost to a relatively bland diet.

One favorite dish of the Ashkenazim that survived the move from the shtetl to North America was the hearty mushroom-potato-barley soup called krupnick. In Europe, krupnick was mostly starchy potatoes seasoned with a little meat and mushroom. Today, rich flanken meat is added in large strips, and mushrooms become the major flavoring ingredient. Potatoes are often replaced by lima beans as well.

Moving with the times, I have taken the delicious beef-based mushroom barley soup from my first book and created a vegetarian version that is just as rich and delicious, and probably more like the original krupnick!

The secret to the thickness of this soup is the lima beans. They are peeled and therefore disintegrate into the stock when fully cooked. Don't panic—they peel very easily when properly soaked and children love to pop them out of their skins.

1¼ cups dried large lima beans

1 ounce (¾ cup loosely packed) dried imported mushrooms, preferably porcini

2 quarts water or packaged vegetable or mushroom broth

1 mushroom bouillon cube (optional)

2 tablespoons extra virgin olive oil or vegetable oil

1 onion, finely diced

1 stalk celery, finely diced

8 ounces white mushrooms, diced

Salt and pepper to taste

1 carrot, diced

½ cup medium pearl barley

---

1. Cover the lima beans in a 2-quart glass bowl with 1 inch of water. Microwave on high for 3 minutes, and then let them soak for 1 or more hours or until the skins easily slide off.

2. Place dried mushrooms in a 1-quart glass bowl and cover with water. Microwave for 2 minutes, and let them sit in the water while you peel the lima beans.

3. Meanwhile, remove the skins from the lima beans by gently squeezing on one end; the bean will just slide out. Place beans in a 4-quart pot.

4. Carefully lift the mushrooms out of the water, and gently squeeze them over the bowl. Save the juices. Chop the soaked mushrooms and set aside.

5. Add the water or broth and the chopped, soaked mushrooms to the lima beans in the pot. Strain the mushroom liquid into the pot as well.

6. Heat a 10-inch frying pan for 20 seconds. Add the oil and heat for 10 seconds. Add the diced onion and sauté for 2 minutes.

7. Add the celery and fresh mushrooms to the pan and cook until wilted and

translucent. Add this mixture to the soup pot along with the diced carrot, and salt and pepper to taste.

8. Cook, covered, over medium heat for 1 hour, stirring occasionally so that the beans do not stick to the pot.

9. Add the barley and cook for ½ hour to 1 hour longer or until the barley is tender and the lima beans disappear. Check the seasoning. Add more broth if the soup is too thick (it will thicken even more when cool).

YIELD: SERVES 6-8

Kitchen Conversations

Mushroom barley soup is a good example of making the most of simple, inexpensive ingredients. Such recipes are often our favorite comfort foods. What's your favorite comfort food? Why?

TINA'S TIDBITS

- *To keep a child's attention and for safety reasons, do steps 1 and 2 before you start the recipe with a young child. Older children can work a recipe in stages, but younger ones work in the present. This is where "soak overnight" is a good step to take!*
- *If you own a pressure cooker, lima beans can be cooked for 15 minutes on low setting, and then they will be ready to peel.*
- *Do not make the mistake of buying small lima beans. It will take you forever to peel them!*
- *Olive oil mimics the taste of traditional goose fat, and sautéing the vegetables adds depth to the flavor of this soup.*

Ethiopian Peanut Soup

Many believe that Ethiopia's Jewish population, the Beta Israel, are the descendants of Solomon and Bathsheba. It has also been suggested that the ancestors of many in the community were from four of the lost tribes of Israel—Dan, Naphtali, Gad, and Asher. In 1622, Christians conquered the Ethiopian Jewish kingdom, and many Jews were killed or sold as slaves. A fragment of the Jewish community still survived in the hills of Ethiopia until the mid 1980s, when life became particularly difficult for Jews fleeing the rebel conflicts at home and living in refugee camps in Sudan. Starting with Operation Moses and continuing with Operation Joshua, Israeli forces evacuated almost sixty-seven hundred Jews from the war-torn lands. By 1990, half of the Jewish Ethiopians lived in Israel, and half lived in Ethiopia. In 1991, Operation Solomon evacuated most of the remaining fourteen thousand Jews and brought them to settle in Israel, ending a twenty-five-hundred-year Jewish presence in Ethiopia. Although Ethiopian Jews living in Israel are granted the rights of full citizenship, their community faces widespread discrimination and socio-economic difficulties. Perhaps attitudes will change now that the first Ethiopian-born Israeli woman has been crowned Miss Israel.

2 chicken breasts, boneless and skinless

Two 10½ ounce cans chicken broth concentrate or 2 quarts pre-made chicken broth

2 onions, peeled and cut into eighths

1 sweet potato, peeled and coarsely chopped

3 carrots, peeled and coarsely chopped

1 cup peanut butter, preferably smooth

⅓ cup long-grain rice (preferably basmati rice)

1½ teaspoons *Berbere* spice (or ½ teaspoon ground coriander, ½ teaspoon nutmeg, ¼ teaspoon cinnamon, mixed)

½ tablespoon kosher salt

3 tablespoons chopped roasted peanuts for garnish (optional)

1. Rinse the chicken breasts in cold water, and then place in a 4-quart pot with the canned chicken broth.

2. Add four cans of water, the onions, sweet potato, and carrots to the other ingredients in the pot. Bring to a boil and then simmer, covered, over moderately low heat for 30 minutes or until the chicken meat is cooked.

3. Remove the chicken from the soup. When cool enough to handle, shred the chicken and set aside.

4. Place about one-third of the soup and the vegetables in an electric blender and blend until very smooth. Place the blended soup in a clean 6-quart pot. Place half or all of the remaining soup into the blender and blend until smooth. Pour into the pot, leaving 1–2 cups in the blender. Add the peanut butter to the remaining soup in the blender and blend until smooth. Add to the pot and bring to a boil.

5. Add the rice, *Berbere* spice or mixed spices, and salt to the pot. Cover and reduce the heat to low. Cook for 20 minutes or until the rice is cooked through.

6. Serve each bowl of soup topped with some shredded chicken meat and a sprinkling of chopped peanuts.

YIELD: SERVES 8-10

Kitchen Conversations

Find Israel and Ethiopia on a map. If Ethiopian Jews are indeed descended from four of the tribes of Israel, how do you think they might have gotten to Ethiopia? What route might they have taken? Imagine the journey. What was different thousands of years later, when the modern Ethiopian Jews came to Israel?

TINA'S TIDBITS

- *When cooking with children, check for sharp edges on soup cans and always completely remove the lid to prevent cuts.*
- *When blending hot liquids, always place a pot holder on top of the closed lid of the blender, pressing down on the lid when you turn the machine on. The force of the hot liquid can push the lid off and scald anyone close by.*
- *As a precaution, never fill the blender container more than two-thirds full so that the hot liquid doesn't seep out.*
- *If you don't have a blender, you can use a food processor. However, process the solids alone first, and then add some of the broth. The soup will not be as smooth as when using a blender, but it will still taste great.*

Potato-Crusted Fish

The holiday of Chanukah tells the story of the rebellion of the Maccabees against the Syrians and the redemption of the Holy Temple, which had been used as a barn and was left filthy and in need of repair. Most Jewish children learn two stories about this uprising: the one-day supply of oil needed to rededicate the eternal light in the Temple that lasted for eight days, and the heroine Judith, who saved her village from an attacking Syrian army. Whether either of these stories really took place at the time of the Maccabees is not as important as that they gave our ancestors hope and encouragement in later times when Jews were being persecuted and prevented from following their religion.

The stories had one lasting effect on Jewish cuisine: fried foods and dairy foods were forever linked to this holiday. The truth is that December is the month in northern countries when all of the fattened geese were slaughtered for their meat to preserve for the winter and their fat rendered for cooking oil. At the same time in the warmer Sephardic lands, the olive crops are being harvested, and fresh pressed olive oil is plentiful.

In the cold regions of northern Europe fish was not the winter choice of protein for Ashkenazim. Fish was always associated with longevity (of the Jewish people) and prosperity and was always served at celebrations. This recipe is my way of bridging the gap between modern tastes and classic holiday celebrations. In addition, one could argue that I have combined the latke with the protein, so just serve the applesauce and sour cream on the side!

1 cup flour
Salt and freshly ground black pepper
    to taste
2 eggs
½ cup buttermilk (or ½ cup milk and
    ½ teaspoon vinegar or lemon juice)
1 or more cups instant potato flakes

Additional salt and freshly ground
    black pepper
6 fillets of mild fish such as tilapia, sole,
    or cod
3 cups olive oil or corn oil

1. Combine the flour with the salt and pepper on a flat dish. Set aside.

2. Beat the eggs with the buttermilk and a pinch of salt in a shallow bowl or soup bowl.

3. Place the potato flakes on a flat plate, and lightly season with some additional salt and pepper.

4. Wash the fish under cold running water, and shake off excess water. Cover each piece of fish with the flour mixture. Shake off any extra flour.

5. Dip the fish in the egg mixture, and then coat completely with the potato flakes, pressing lightly to make sure they stick.

6. Heat the oil in an electric frying pan to 375°F or place in a deep-sided 12-inch frying pan.

7. Submerge the fish in the oil and cook for 2–3 minutes or until golden. Drain on crumpled paper towels, and serve with sour cream, ketchup, or homemade tartar sauce.

YIELD: 4 SERVINGS

TARTAR SAUCE

1 cup regular mayonnaise (not light)
1 tablespoon minced onion
1 tablespoon pickle relish
1 tablespoon minced green olive
 (optional)
1 tablespoon tarragon vinegar

1. Whisk the mayonnaise in a 1-quart mixing bowl.

2. Add the remaining ingredients and stir to combine.

3. Refrigerate until ready to serve with the fish.

TINA'S TIDBITS

- *Preparing the fish is easy with children of all ages. You might want to consider putting the seasoned flour and seasoned potato flakes into gallon plastic storage bags, so that the fish can be shaken in each bag, making for less mess when cooking with very young children.*

- *It goes without saying that frying requires extra precautions. Children must be at waist height to the frying pan, and with children under the age of six, I stand next to them with my arm around their waists to keep them steady and also be able to whisk them away rapidly if I think they are in danger or getting fidgety.*

- *You can fry in less oil, but either gently push the oil in the pan in waves over the top of the fish to get it to cook evenly or turn the fish fillets over after a minute or two.*

- *Fillets cook very fast because they are thin, so judge doneness by the color of the potato crust: when it's golden brown, the fish is good to go.*

Kitchen Conversations

- Why do some holidays last longer than one day? Why is Chanukah celebrated for eight days? What other holidays are celebrated for eight days?

- Could you make fried mozzarella sticks this way too? Try it. You could take care of two food traditions for Chanukah using the same recipe!

Roasted Butternut Squash with Apples and Onions

*T*his recipe may not be a traditional Jewish dish, but I created it in a way that my ancestors in Lithuania and Poland would have done.

Shabbat, holidays, and weddings all inspired cooks to transform their basic food into something more elaborate. In Eastern Europe, squash, apples, and onions were stored all winter in cold home cellars. Adding an onion to a recipe was a normal occurrence. But adding an apple with its sweetness elevated the dish to something special.

Butternut squash is an ideal winter vegetable because it ripens in early fall but its hard skin allows it to be stored and eaten all winter long. Here I combine sweet and savory produce and seasonings to make a great side dish or even a main course served with pasta or a grain.

1 large onion

2 Fuji, Honeycrisp, or Jonagold apples

20 ounces pre-cut butternut squash
   (about 4–5 cups of 1-inch cubes)

3 tablespoons extra virgin olive oil

1 teaspoon dried thyme

1 tablespoon balsamic vinegar

Kosher salt to taste

20 grindings of black pepper or to
   taste

½ teaspoon ground cinnamon

½ cup dried cranberries

¼ cup toasted almond slivers or
   sunflower seeds (optional)

1. Preheat oven to 350°F.

2. Cut the onion in half, and then slice each piece crosswise into ½-inch strips. Place on a large rimmed baking sheet covered with parchment paper or foil (dull side up). Set aside.

3. Using an apple corer/slicer, cut the apples into eighths, and then cut each wedge into 3 or 4 chunks. Add to the onions along with the squash cubes.

4. Add the oil, thyme, vinegar, salt, and pepper to the baking sheet and toss well.

5. Spread out in a single layer, and bake for 30 minutes or until the onions are golden and the squash is tender when pierced with a fork.

6. Remove from the oven. Sprinkle with the cinnamon, dried cranberries, and nuts (if using). Toss lightly and place in a serving dish.

YIELD: 6–8 SERVINGS AS A SIDE DISH

- *Since some apples are very hard, placing your hands next to, or on top of the child's hand while pressing down will be useful—but don't press too hard on their little hands if the apple is very hard!*
- *It is much safer to use an 8-inch chef's knife with a child under 6 than a paring or utility knife. Standing behind the child and holding the knife with him or her instills confidence at the same time that you focus on safety.*
- *Combining the cranberries and apples with the savory vegetables makes the dish more intriguing for young children and will promote eating a new, healthy vegetable.*
- *This dish is perfect as a side dish for chicken or fish. However, serve this dish on top of quinoa or barley and you will have a nutritious vegetarian main dish.*

Kitchen Conversations

● How many colors are in this dish? Which ingredients are fruits and which are vegetables?

● Since you didn't add sugar to the dish, what makes the onions and squash sweeter?

Sweet Potato and Carrot Latkes

*W*hen I was the food columnist for Reform Judaism *magazine, a reader who followed a strict gluten-free diet wrote to me looking for traditional Chanukah recipes that she could eat. Because she couldn't eat flour or matzah meal, most potato pancake recipes were out, so I created this recipe, as both a gluten-free alternative to traditional latkes and as a tribute to the Beta Israel Ethiopian Jewish community.*

The flavors in this dish are commonly found in Ethiopian cooking. Teff is the smallest cultivated grain in the world; it grows in the mountains of Ethiopia and also happens to be gluten-free. It has a mild, slightly molasses-like sweetness that goes well with many vegetables besides those in this recipe. Ground teff seeds are the basis for injera bread, the spongy, slightly sour, soft flatbread that is used as plate and fork and eaten at Ethiopian meals.

Teff can be found in many supermarkets, especially those oriented toward natural foods, as well as in most health-food stores. As an alternative, I suggest ground flaxseed, which will also help the latkes hold together. This is a high-nutrient dish that could easily serve as an entrée with fruit sauce and Greek yogurt or sour cream. Kids love the color and taste too!

1 pound sweet potatoes, peeled
½ pound carrots, peeled
1 small onion, cut into eighths
1 large clove garlic, cut into 3 pieces
1 teaspoon salt or to taste
15 grindings of black pepper
½ teaspoon powdered ginger
½ teaspoon dried oregano or ½

tablespoon chopped fresh oregano
½ teaspoon dried basil or ½ tablespoon chopped fresh basil
2 large eggs
¼ to ⅓ cup teff or ground flaxseed
Canola or peanut oil for frying
Greek yogurt or sour cream for garnish (optional)

1. Cut the sweet potatoes and carrots into 1½-inch chunks, and grate them using the fine grating disk on a processor. Empty the mixture into a 3-quart bowl.

2. Place the onion and garlic pieces in the food processor work bowl fitted with the metal blade. Pulse the machine on and off until the onions are finely chopped. Return half of the potato/carrot mixture to the processor work bowl, and pulse on and off about 5 times to combine the ingredients. Empty the work bowl into the mixing bowl with remaining potato/carrot mixture.

3. Add the spices, the eggs, and ¼ cup of the teff or ground flaxseed to the mixing bowl, and mix thoroughly. Add a little more grain if the mixture seems too loose and watery. Do not make the mixture too firm or the finished product will be dry and heavy.

4. Heat a large skillet or griddle on high heat for 20 seconds. Add enough oil to totally cover the bottom of the pan. Heat the oil for 10 seconds. If the oil begins to smoke, reduce the heat to medium-high.

5. Drop 2 tablespoons of the potato-carrot mixture into the hot pan using a food scoop or spoon. Each time before you scoop up some of the latke batter, stir the contents of the bowl. Repeat with more mixture to fill the pan, but do not overcrowd.

6. When the bottoms of the pancakes are golden, gently turn them over using two slotted spatulas. When golden on the second side, remove to a plate that is covered with crumpled paper towels.

7. Proceed with the remaining mixture.

8. Serve plain or with a dollop of sour cream or Greek yogurt.

YIELD: 2 DOZEN LATKES

Kitchen Conversations

● Talk about the story of Chanukah and its use of oil. Do you think Ethiopians told this story to their children? Why or why not?

● What other vegetables can you add in place of the potato or carrot to create your own holiday treat? Write it down and start your own Chanukah tradition.

TINA'S TIDBITS

• *Children of all ages can help make the batter for the latkes, but only children over the age of eight or nine should be allowed to fry the pancakes. Since this mixture has so much natural moisture, there is a stronger likelihood that the oil will splatter. Only taller children should be allowed to work at the stove. Younger children can watch, but **not** sitting on the countertop nearby.*

• *Using the grating disk on a food processor guarantees no nicked knuckles. However, do pay attention to make sure the feed tube plunger is used!*

Zimsterne Cookies

J ewish cooks often modified recipes from the surrounding non-Jewish communities and created their own dishes to be served at festive occasions. Zimsterne cookies are a perfect example of this transformation. The original zimsterne cookies were cinnamon meringue stars served at Christmastime, but German Jews adapted that recipe and served them at the end of Yom Kippur.

Eastern European Jews did not have the money or time to make these delicate nut cookies, so they created their own star-shaped cookies (zimsterne means "stars") for Shabbat and holiday platters of sweets that were soft and chewy and made with honey and spices. These cookies were similar to the gingerbread men that were also made at Christmastime. Adapting this recipe for Purim, German Jewish children would pretend that the cookie was Haman and would bite off its head!

4 tablespoons unsalted butter	½ teaspoon salt
1 cup sugar	1 teaspoon cinnamon
3 large eggs	½ teaspoon cloves
½ cup honey	½ teaspoon ginger
1 teaspoon vanilla	Confectioners' sugar for rolling the
5 cups all-purpose flour	dough
¾ teaspoon baking soda	

Decorative Icing:

1 cup confectioners' sugar
¼ teaspoon vanilla
1–2 tablespoons milk

1. Cream the butter and the sugar together with an electric mixer until light and fluffy. Add the eggs, and beat until the mixture gets lighter in color. Beat in the honey and vanilla.

2. Mix the baking soda and spices with 1 cup of the flour. Set aside.

3. With the mixer on low speed, gradually add the remaining 4 cups of flour, mixing well to form a thick dough. If your mixer is powerful, use it to add the reserved cup of flour and spices until well combined. If not, stir the remaining flour into the dough by hand. Make sure that the mixture is thoroughly combined.

4. Pat the dough into a flat round, and place in a plastic storage bag. Seal and store in the refrigerator for 1 hour or until firm and easy to handle.

5. Preheat the oven to 300°F. Lightly dust a pastry board with some confectioners' sugar. Roll the dough out on the board to ¼-inch thickness.

6. Cut the dough into star shapes using a cookie cutter, and place on a cookie sheet lined with parchment paper. Bake for 15 minutes or until golden. Allow the cookies to cool for 5–10 minutes while you make the icing.

7. To make the icing: Place the cup of confectioners' sugar in a 1-quart mixing bowl. Whisk in the vanilla and 1 tablespoon of the milk until smooth. If the mixture is too thick, whisk in some more milk until the mixture resembles mayonnaise in consistency.

8. Using a pastry brush, brush the icing over the tops of the warm cookies and let sit at room temperature until the cookies are cool and the icing is dry and no longer sticky. Store in an airtight container at room temperature, or freeze until later use.

YIELD: 3-4 DOZEN COOKIES

Kitchen Conversations

● Can you tell one spice from another without looking? Close your eyes and have someone open a spice jar. Smell it. Do you know what it is?

● Do you have a favorite spice?

TINA'S TIDBITS

- *Children love to cut out cookies and transfer them to the cookie sheet. A trick to prevent the dough from dragging on the spatula and losing its shape is to rub a scrap of dough on the spatula and then dip the spatula in some of the confectioners' sugar before you transfer the cookie onto the baking sheet.*
- *Using a rolling pin is often challenging for young hands. However, rolling pin bands of varying thickness are sold that fit on the ends of the rolling pin to ensure the dough isn't rolled unevenly.*

BARLEY SALAD WITH FRESH HERBS
AND POMEGRANATE DRESSING, PAGE 38

Spring

Early spring in the Jewish community focuses on the rebirth of the earth and the life of the Jewish community through the celebrations of Purim and Passover. There are so many food traditions and recipes associated with Passover that they can be found in their own section in this book. It is thought that Purim and Passover are connected by one tradition related to food, the *shalach manos* (Yiddish) or *shalach manot* or *mishlo-ach manot* (Hebrew) baskets. By making baked gifts for Purim, households could use their remaining flour and other baking ingredients to rid the kitchen of chametz before they began the thorough cleaning of the house for Passover.

Preparing and gifting foods for Purim provides opportunities beyond the joy of creating together in the kitchen. At Purim it is considered a mitzvah to give gifts to the less fortunate. Tradition dictates that there should be at least two different gifts of food and that they should be given directly to two separate people who are poor. Giving *tzedakah* is one of the tenets of Judaism, which is why it was the custom to have the children distribute the food gifts: it's a perfect opportunity to teach empathy and responsibility toward other people.

In addition to baking and cooking items for the gifts, children and adults can also get involved by decorating paper plates or baskets for the food.

Spring is also the season when many baby animals are born, which is why there is an abundance of milk and dairy products at this time. Dairy foods are therefore associated with the holiday of Shavuot. In biblical times Shavuot was a harvest festival, but after the destruction of the Holy Temple in Jerusalem in 70 CE, the early Rabbis shifted the focus of the holiday to the giving of the Torah. Because certain foods like blintzes or manicotti resemble the scrolls of the Torah, it has become a custom to serve these and other tubular foods for Shavuot.

Beet Hummus

Say *"beets" in the Jewish community and people often think of borscht, that slightly sweet/tart, cold soup, whose bright magenta color morphs into pastel only when a dollop of sour cream is added. Beets were a cheap and plentiful tuber abundant in Eastern Europe and Ukraine (the word* borsch *refers to soup of any kind in Ukraine) and became a staple of the impoverished Jewish and Polish communities. In most temperate climates, beets were harvested in summer and early fall and stored all winter in root cellars.*

Hummus, the mixture of chickpeas and sesame paste, originated in the Middle East and could probably be considered an Israeli national dish, because it is served at all meals and festive occasions. A few years ago I was served beet hummus at an upscale restaurant in Tel Aviv. The following is my interpretation of this delicious dish and a great way to introduce children to beets.

One 15-ounce can whole beets, rinsed
   and drained
One 15-ounce can chickpeas (garbanzo
   beans), rinsed and drained
¼ cup tahini (sesame butter)
2 tablespoons lemon juice
2 tablespoons extra virgin olive oil

2 cloves of garlic
1 teaspoon ground cumin
¼ teaspoon *baharat*, or cinnamon or
   allspice and a pinch of cayenne
1 teaspoon kosher salt
10 grindings of black pepper or to taste

1. Place drained beets and garbanzo beans in a food processor work bowl, and *pulse* the machine on and off until the two ingredients are blended into a coarse texture. Scrape down the sides of the work bowl with a rubber spatula.

2. Add the remaining ingredients, and process until the ingredients form a fairly smooth paste.

3. Place the mixture in a decorative bowl, and serve with pita bread or vegetables for dipping.

YIELD: 1 PINT

- *As an alternative to canned beets, this recipe may be made with one large, fresh beet that has been oven roasted and peeled.*
- *When pulsing the processor, incorporate counting skills. Count each time the child presses down on the button. A machine that is to be turned on for 5 seconds can be timed by calling out "one-100, two-100," and so on.*
- *Baharat is a mixture of spices whose use originated in India but is widely used in the Middle East. Different mixtures of spices are found in different regions, but cinnamon, cumin, cloves, and sometimes pepper or lemony sumac are most often included as the basis for this mixture. Cinnamon or allspice can be substituted for this recipe.*
- *Do not substitute peanut butter for the tahini in this recipe. Peanut butter and peanut oil are so distinctive in flavor that they rarely can be substituted for other butters or oils called for in a recipe.*

Kitchen Conversations

- One variety of beets is grown only to produce sugar. The largest of these crops are found in Russia and Poland. Did any of your ancestors come from that region of the world?

- Is sugar sometimes added to meat or vegetable dishes in your family's recipes? Do you think there is a connection?

Barley Salad with Fresh Herbs and Pomegranate Dressing

W hen the Holy Temple still stood in Jerusalem, Jews from all over the Land of Israel would come to Jerusalem for three major festivals—Pesach, Shavuot, and Sukkot. These three holidays all centered on harvest times of the year. Although the story of Passover has always focused on our escape from slavery in Egypt, it also celebrated the first crop of spring, barley.

Although today's custom prevents us from eating any barley during the days of Pesach, in ancient times Jews would eat barley after the first seder was conducted. This salad highlights the new barley and fresh herbs that grow during spring in Israel.

1½ cups pearled barley
½ cup dried sweetened cranberries
¼ cup orange juice
3 stalks of celery
3 tablespoons chopped fresh dill

2 tablespoons chopped parsley
2 tablespoons chiffonade of basil
Seeds from ½ fresh pomegranate or 25
    medium seedless red grapes cut into
    quarters (about ½ cup)

Dressing:

3 tablespoons extra virgin olive oil
2 tablespoons rice wine vinegar
1 teaspoon pomegranate molasses
1 teaspoon allspice
½ teaspoon cinnamon
1 teaspoon kosher salt
15 grindings of black pepper
    (¼ teaspoon)

1. Place barley in a pressure cooker and cover with 1½ quarts of water. Cook on pressure #1 for 20 minutes or follow manufacturer's directions. Alternatively, cook barley and water in a covered 3-quart saucepan over moderate heat for 45 minutes or until tender but not mushy. Drain and rinse barley in a colander, and place barley in a large mixing bowl.

2. Microwave dried cranberries and orange juice on high for 45 seconds. Set aside.

3. Cut celery stalks in half lengthwise, and then slice stalks into ¼-inch pieces. Add to the barley.

4. Chop dill and parsley with a chef's knife, and chiffonade the basil with the same knife. Use a paring knife to cut the grapes (if using). Add herbs, pomegranate seeds or grapes, and dried sweetened cranberries to the barley. Set aside or refrigerate while you make the dressing.

5. Put the dressing ingredients in a screw-top jar. Cover and shake well to combine.

6. Pour some dressing over the barley salad, and toss gently with a rubber spatula or wooden spoon until it is moistened but not soupy. Reserve any remaining dressing for later if the salad seems dry.

YIELD: 6-8 SERVINGS

Kitchen Conversations

● Is there some fruit or vegetable that is ripe now that would be a good substitute for an ingredient in the barley salad? Would you have to change some spice or other ingredient to have the salad taste good?

● Take a trip to the supermarket and introduce the child to the produce department. Identify items that are familiar and new to the child.

TINA'S TIDBITS

• *Regardless of the age of the child, I would suggest the barley be cooked before you engage him or her in making this recipe.*

• *Fresh pomegranates are not always available, so I have included the delicious alternative of seedless red grapes.*

• *All children can make this recipe but children under the age of 7 do not have to have the coordination to use a paring knife if using the grapes.*

Manicotti with Tomato Sauce

Manicotti is a great symbolic dish to serve for Shavuot; it contains cheese—a traditional ingredient for Shavuot celebrations—and it is tubular in shape, to mimic the scrolls of the Torah. Perhaps Jewish Italian cooks also saw this connection and made manicotti for Shavuot? If they did, this tradition didn't start until the 1500s, when tomatoes began to be eaten in Italy and other parts of Europe.

Tomatoes are part of the nightshade family, and many people thought they were poisonous. However, perhaps some adventurous person decided to try a tomato, and when he didn't get sick or die, people started to grow the tomato, which is actually a fruit, not a vegetable. Jewish cooks were quick to adapt the tomato into their cooking and new culinary traditions were born.

SAUCE:

4 tablespoons extra virgin olive oil
1 onion, finely chopped
2 cloves garlic, minced
2 tablespoons chopped parsley
One 28-ounce can recipe-ready
   crushed tomatoes
One 8-ounce can tomato sauce
Salt and freshly ground black pepper
   to taste
1 tablespoon chopped fresh basil or
   1 teaspoon dried
1 teaspoon or more sugar, if needed

MANICOTTI:

1 box manicotti shells
1 pound ricotta cheese, part skim or
   whole milk
8 ounces mozzarella, diced into ¼-inch
   cubes
⅓ cup freshly grated Parmesan cheese
¼ cup finely chopped parsley
2 teaspoons sugar
2 large eggs, beaten with a fork
Salt and freshly ground black pepper
   to taste
Generous pinch of nutmeg

1. To make the sauce, heat a 3-quart saucepan over high heat for 15 seconds. Add the olive oil and heat for 10 seconds. Add the onions to the hot oil and sauté for 3 minutes. Add the garlic and sauté the mixture until lightly golden. Do not allow the garlic to burn or the sauce will be bitter.

2. Add the remaining sauce ingredients and simmer uncovered for 20–30 minutes or until the sauce is thick.

3. Meanwhile, cook the manicotti shells according to package directions. Drain in a colander. Place the shells in a 2-quart bowl, and pour cold water over the shells. Leave the shells in the water while you make the filling.

4. Combine all of the ingredients for the filling in a bowl.

5. Place a large, plain decorating tip (#6) into a 14-inch pastry bag. Fold the top of the bag downward to create a 4-inch cuff around the top of the bag. Rest the bag in your hand with your fingers underneath the cuff and the tip touching the countertop. Spoon the filling into the bag. Unfold the cuff. Bring the top edges of the bag together, and pleat them

closed so no filling oozes out the top. Place the bag in the crook between your thumb and forefinger, and twist the bag until the cheese mixture tightly fills the bag near the tip.

6. Holding a drained manicotti shell in your other hand, place the tip of the bag inside of the shell and squeeze while you slowly pull the bag out of the pasta shell, filling the tube from the center out. Turn the shell around, and fill the remaining half of the pasta.

7. Place some of the sauce in a 13 x 9-inch baking dish. As you fill the manicotti shells, place them in the dish. When all the manicotti are filled, pour the remaining sauce on top, sprinkle with extra Parmesan cheese, and bake for 30 minutes at 350°F or until bubbling.

YIELD: 6-8 SERVINGS

Kitchen Conversations

● Did you know that Jews have lived in Italy for over two thousand years? They are not called Ashkenazim or Sephardim. They are called Italkim.

● Search the Internet for Italian Jews, and see pictures of the Roman Ghetto and the Venetian Ghettos. Find out how "ghetto" got its name!

● What other foods could look like the Torah on our plates?

TINA'S TIDBITS

• *If you don't have a pastry bag and tip, the cheese filling can be placed in a gallon ziplock bag. Seal the bag, push all the filling to one corner of the bag, and cut out a ½-inch point. Fill the pasta tube as described above.*

• *Here are two suggestions for making this recipe with young children or for older children who want to make this dish independently:*

  1. *Have the child hold the pasta tube while you or another child fills the manicotti.*
  2. *Jumbo pasta shells can be used in place of manicotti tubes. Older children will find the shells easily filled by squeezing the shells open and filling with a spoon.*

Grandma Lucille's Blintz Soufflé

I recently found my mother's handwritten recipe for blintz soufflé. Not only was it a reminder of a delicious dish, but seeing her handwriting evoked wonderful memories. This feeling reinforced my belief that our recipes connect us to our past and our history and that this connection must be kept vibrant. This dish is included not only for your enjoyment but for her grandchildren's enjoyment as well.

Blintzes are a popular dish for many Jewish celebrations, but they are most often served to celebrate Shavuot. Eating dairy products is linked with this holiday for many reasons. Some believe that when the laws were given at Mount Sinai (which Shavuot commemorates), no kosher meat was available so the people ate dairy foods to fulfill the laws of kashrut. Another, more likely, theory is that the animals gave birth in the spring (when Shavuot is celebrated), and milk from cows and sheep was plentiful for making cheese and other dairy-based dishes. Blintzes in particular make for an ideal holiday treat because two blintzes side by side on a plate will look like the two sides of a Torah scroll.

I've never been able to find mention of blintz soufflé in cookbooks published prior to the 1970s. It is possible that the incorporation of the Golden Company in 1978 and the instant popularity of its line of blintzes had a lot to do with the timing of the birth of the blintz soufflé. My version comes from one in my collection written in my mother's handwriting in the late 1970s.

1 stick unsalted butter
1 dozen cheese or fruit-filled blintzes
   (homemade or frozen)
4 eggs
1½ cups sour cream or Greek yogurt

¼ cup sugar
½ teaspoon salt
1 teaspoon vanilla
1 tablespoon orange juice

1. Preheat oven to 350°F.

2. Microwave the butter directly in a 13 x 9-inch glass baking dish until melted. Place the blintzes over the butter in one layer.

3. Meanwhile, whisk the four eggs in a 2-quart mixing bowl. Add the remaining ingredients and blend well. Pour over the blintzes.

4. Bake for 35–45 minutes or until the top starts to brown. Cut along each blintz or into squares.

YIELD: 12+ SERVINGS

TINA'S TIDBITS

• This recipe is delicious and easy to make with young children. However, after you melt the butter in the casserole, let the dish cool so that no little hands are burned.

• Homemade applesauce (see page 14) would be a light accompaniment to this dish if cheese blintzes are used instead of fruit-filled blintzes.

Kitchen Conversations

● Blintzes were originally made in Ukraine, which was part of the Pale of Settlement, an area that included parts of modern-day Russia, Ukraine, Lithuania, and other countries, where Jews of the Russian Empire were forced to live for almost 150 years. Many North American Jewish families (including mine) trace their roots to this part of the world. Where did your ancestors come from? Did people in your family grow up eating blintzes?

● What are your favorite dairy foods?

Chocolate Chip Mystery Mandelbrot

Mandelbrot *means "almond bread" in Yiddish, but its origins are the biscotti cookies that were created in Italy over seven hundred years ago. These biscotti originally contained no fat or sugar and were baked twice so that they would be very hard and dry and last for months on ships at sea. Biscotti recipes traveled north to Germany, where they became very popular with the Jewish community because they could be made in advance of Shabbat and stay fresh for days.*

Around the early 1900s, oil or butter was added to the dough, along with different nuts, dried fruit, or chocolate chips, and our modern mandelbrot *was created. During the Depression and World War II, butter and cooking oil were expensive and hard to come by, so mayonnaise was often used in their place. Mayonnaise is the secret ingredient in these mystery* mandelbrot.

Hellmann's mayonnaise was created by Nina Hellmann in 1905 to use on sandwiches and for sale in her German husband's deli in New York City. Perhaps the Hellmanns were Jewish? Who knows, but Hellmann's mayonnaise makes these cookies delicious!

The almond tree is the first tree to bloom in Israel in the early spring, making this recipe perfect for TuBiSh'vat.

1. Preheat the oven to 325°F.

2. Place the flour, sugar, baking powder, and cinnamon in a 3-quart mixing bowl and stir with a wooden spoon to combine.

3. Add the remaining ingredients and mix thoroughly.

4. Divide the dough in half and form into 2 long, narrow loaves on a cookie sheet lined with parchment paper. Bake for 25 minutes. Remove the cookie sheet from the oven and cool 5 minutes.

1½ cups flour	⅓ cup Hellmann's mayonnaise
¾ cup sugar	2 teaspoons vanilla extract
1 teaspoon baking powder	1 cup semisweet chocolate chips,
½ teaspoon cinnamon	regular or mini variety
2 eggs, lightly beaten	½ cup slivered almonds

5. Carefully transfer one loaf to a cutting board. Using a chef's knife, slice the loaf on the diagonal into ½-inch slices. Lay the slices cut side down on the cookie sheet, and repeat with the other loaf. Return the cookie sheet to the oven and bake for 5 minutes.

6. Remove the cookie sheet from the oven, turn the slices over, and return to the oven to bake for another 5 minutes or until golden. Cool completely before storing in a sealed container.

YIELD: ABOUT 3 DOZEN SLICES

Kitchen Conversations

Look at the label on the jar of mayonnaise and read the list of ingredients. Discuss why it makes the cookies taste so good and light. What other recipes could use mayonnaise instead of oil?

TINA'S TIDBITS

- *This recipe is perfect for children of all ages because no electrical equipment is necessary and the dough is easy to work with.*
- *An adult should transfer the hot loaves to a cutting board, but after 5 minutes, supervised children can use a chef's knife to cut the dough into slices.*
- *Only children over the age of seven or eight should be allowed to turn the hot slices over, because the cookie sheet is very hot.*

Gluten-Free Hamantaschen Dough (Dairy)

Hamantaschen, or "Haman's pockets," are the traditional Purim dessert of Ashkenazic Jews. Hamantaschen originally contained poppy seed filling in medieval Germany, but it later became popular to fill the hamantaschen with prune filling in honor of a Jewish prune-jam merchant named David Brandeis, who was set free after being falsely accused of poisoning a magistrate. His community in Bohemia (now part of the Czech Republic) celebrated by filling hamantaschen with his jam. Today hamantaschen are filled with many different flavors of fruit jams, nuts, and even chocolate.

A reader of my food column in Reform Judaism magazine once requested hamantaschen dough that her child, who couldn't eat gluten, could enjoy. Gluten is a protein found in many grains, including wheat, barley, and rye, to which some people are allergic or especially sensitive, and eating foods that contain gluten makes them feel sick. Here is a recipe that my reader's child or any child can eat and enjoy.

---

1 stick unsalted butter
¾ cup sugar
2 large eggs
1½ teaspoons vanilla extract
½ teaspoon pure almond extract
2 cups gluten-free flour plus ¼ cup for kneading

1 teaspoon baking powder
½ teaspoon salt
Confectioners' sugar
Filling of your choice or homemade gluten-free chocolate filling (see page 48)

---

1. Preheat oven to 350°F. Line cookie sheets with parchment paper.

2. Using an electric mixer, cream the butter and sugar together until thoroughly combined.

3. Add the eggs and vanilla and almond extracts, and beat until lighter in color and fluffy.

4. Combine the 2 cups flour, baking powder, and salt in a 1-quart bowl. Add to the mixer bowl, and mix on medium speed just until the dough starts to hold together.

5. On a surface lightly floured with the additional ¼ cup flour, very gently knead the dough about ten strokes or until the dough is smooth and holds together. Cover with plastic wrap, flatten into a disk, and refrigerate for at least 30 minutes.

6. Place the dough between two sheets of parchment paper or waxed paper that have been lightly dusted with confectioners' sugar. Roll the dough out to about ¼-inch thickness. Carefully remove one sheet of paper (you might have to scrape some of the dough off if it sticks) and then place dough side down on a board that is heavily covered with confectioners' sugar.

7. Carefully remove the paper on top. If necessary, dust with additional confectioners' sugar, and lightly roll to make the surface uniform in thickness. (NOTE: This is necessary only if the dough was very sticky and pulled apart when removing the paper.)

8. Cut the dough into 2½-inch circles.

9. Transfer each dough circle with a small spatula to an area on your board that has also been coated with confectioner's sugar. Coat your fingers as well. Place 1 scant teaspoon of filling in the center of each circle.

10. Using your thumbs and forefingers, shape the hamantaschen. Imagine the circle is a clock; place your two thumbs at 6and your forefingers at 2 and 10. Gently bring your fingers together and you will form perfect hamantaschen!

11. Pinch the dough together so that the filling is exposed only at the center of the cookie.

12. Bake the hamantaschen in the preheated oven for 10 minutes or until golden. Remove from the oven and cool completely. Store in a plastic bag or container, or freeze for later use.

YIELD: ABOUT 18 HAMANTASCHEN

TINA'S TIDBITS

- *This dough is much harder to work with than regular cookie dough. I wouldn't make this recipe with a very young child for that reason. However, every attempt should be made to let children with gluten allergies enjoy this holiday tradition.*

- *Because there is no gluten in this recipe, the dough relies only on the eggs for structure, which makes the dough more moist and harder to handle. Heavily coating your fingers and work surface with confectioners' sugar will make the dough less sticky and easier to handle.*

- *Chilled dough is more firm if it is made with butter, so I recommend using butter for this recipe. However, if you want pareve cookies, consider using coconut oil (which is solid at room temperature) or a firm margarine in its place.*

Kitchen Conversations

● Most of the Jewish world eats different pastries on Purim to represent Haman. Explore other traditions, or talk about special foods you eat for Purim.

● *Shalach manot* baskets are filled with treats and brought to friends for Purim. Decorate a basket, and place hamantaschen, candies, and fruits in the basket to give to someone special.

● Did you know there is a theory that giving *shalach manot* baskets was a way to use up flour and other foods around the house that would not be allowed for Passover? Discuss this and see what foods are in your kitchen that would be good to use in your gift basket.

Chocolate Filling for Hamantaschen (Gluten-Free)

P oppy seed filling for hamantaschen is said to represent the vegetarian diet of nuts and seeds Queen Esther ate in King Ahasuerus's court, refusing to eat nonkosher meat while hiding her Jewish identity from the king.

There is no special symbolism to the chocolate other than the fact that it is a popular filling today. However, did you know that it was a Jewish man by the name of Benjamin d'Acosta de Andrade who, in the late 1600s on the island of Curaçao, invented a process that would prepare cacao beans to use in beverages and pastries? This allowed cacao to be shipped all over the world ready to be made into wonderful treats!

¾ stick of unsalted butter

3 ounces chocolate chips + 1-ounce square unsweetened chocolate or 3.5-ounce bar of 78% cacao

¾ cup granulated sugar

1½ teaspoons vanilla extract

½ teaspoon almond extract

¼ teaspoon salt

2 large eggs

1 tablespoon rice flour

---

1. Place the butter and chocolate in a 1½-quart glass mixing bowl and microwave on 80 percent for 45 seconds; if the butter is not completely melted, then heat on high for an additional 15 seconds. Stir the contents of the bowl until smooth.

2. Whisk the sugar, vanilla and almond extracts, and salt into the chocolate mixture. Combine well to dissolve some of the sugar.

3. Add eggs one at a time, whisking well after each addition.

4. Add the rice flour and whisk until a smooth, shiny mass forms in the center of the bowl.

5. Place the mixture in a sealed container, and refrigerate until needed. The filling will become firm but not too firm to scoop into little mounds for filling the hamantaschen.

TINA'S TIDBITS

- *This recipe is good for all ages, although little ones might need some help whisking the mixture when it becomes thick.*
- *Make sure the microwave oven is below eye level for the child. If not, an adult must remove the hot bowl to prevent burns.*
- *Chocolate often retains its shape when melted, so don't be fooled and check at different intervals according to the directions above.*
- *If gluten is not a concern and you don't have rice flour at home, you can substitute 2 tablespoons all-purpose flour for the 1 tablespoon rice flour.*
- *Alternatively, if you use 1 tablespoon potato starch instead of flour, the filling could be used in Passover pastries!*

Kitchen Conversations

- Gluten is the protein found in wheat flour. Some people have allergies to gluten and get bad stomachaches if they eat it. Rice flour doesn't contain gluten, so this filling is safe to eat for those who follow a gluten-free diet. Can you think of other fillings for hamantaschen that would be safe as well?

- Look on the labels of canned fillings. Do you think they are gluten-free? Would they be okay to use?

- Do you have a friend who can't have gluten? Talk about the foods he or she can and cannot eat so that the next time you play together you can have (or even make) snacks that both of you can share.

Almond Poppy Seed Pound Cake

I n 1925, the Solo Company started manufacturing pastry fillings, and the first two produced were prune filling and poppyseed—the same fillings that Jewish people traditionally used to fill their hamantaschen. I don't think the owner was Jewish, but Mr. Sokol was from Bohemia, where the first prune hamantaschen were made!

I created this recipe one Purim. After making all of my hamantaschen, I found myself with a little leftover filling in each can. What to do? Make a delicious pound cake, which is still a family favorite!

---

1 cup unsalted butter
1¼ cup sugar
½ cup canned poppy seed pastry filling
½ cup canned apricot or almond pastry filling
¼ teaspoon almond extract
1 teaspoon vanilla extract

4 eggs
1 cup low-fat, thick Greek yogurt
2½ cups all-purpose flour
1 teaspoon baking soda
1 teaspoon salt

---

1. Preheat oven to 350°F.

2. Lightly spray 4 mini loaf pans or 1 large Bundt pan with cooking spray or lightly grease with vegetable oil. Set aside.

3. Cream the butter and sugar together on high speed with an electric mixer until light and fluffy.

4. Add poppy seed filling, apricot or almond filling, almond extract, and vanilla extract to butter mixture, and mix at medium speed until all ingredients are well combined.

5. Add eggs and beat at medium speed until mixture is lighter in color and aerated.

6. Add the yogurt and mix on medium speed until well incorporated.

7. In a 1-quart bowl, stir the flour, baking soda, and salt together. Add this mixture to the mixing bowl and mix on low speed just until the batter is well combined. Scrape the batter from the sides of the bowl with a rubber spatula.

8. Pour the batter evenly into 4 prepared mini loaf pans placed on a low-rimmed cookie sheet or into one large Bundt pan, and bake for 40 to 60 minutes (depending on the size of the pan) until a toothpick inserted into the center of the cake comes out clean.

9. Let the cakes cool for 5 minutes. Then remove the cakes from the pans and place on a cooling rack. Cool thoroughly before covering or freezing for later use.

YIELD: 20 SERVINGS

- *Children love to make cakes, but many a little finger has been caught in the mixer paddle when no one was looking!* **Never** *leave a child unattended by an electric mixer if he or she can reach the on/off switch. If you must retrieve an ingredient—even if it is close by—unplug the machine.*

- *Step stools are important while cooking but especially when working at a counter. Children need to see what is happening in the bowl, so make sure they are high enough to see. They should be standing, not sitting on the counter!*

- *If you are using a handheld mixer, make sure both of the child's hands are on top holding the mixer. This way all fingers are accounted for, and the child has more control over guiding the mixer around the bowl.*

- *With children around four or five years old, hold your hands over theirs while using the mixer. They do not have the strength to hold it, and this way you can protect them from dropping a turned-on mixer and have a wonderful time cooking together.*

Kitchen Conversations

● Look up the region of Bohemia on a map. Today Bohemia is part of the Czech Republic, but it has been part of several countries over the last hundred years. Where do your ancestors come from? Has the city or region always been in the same country? How do you think the map would look different if we drew borders by food traditions?

● The Bohemian town of Jungbunzlau is where prune-filled hamantaschen were invented, in honor of David Brandeis, the prune-jam merchant who was accused of poisoning a magistrate but was found innocent. Today the town is also known by its Czech name, Mladá Boleslav. Find it on a map. Now find the city of Pilsen where Mr. Sokol came from. Are the cities near each other?

GREEN TEA–JASMINE SORBET WITH
ASSORTED FRUITS, PAGE 68

Summer

There are no Jewish festivals celebrated during the hot summer months, but the fresh peaches, plums, melons, berries, cherries, corn, cucumbers, tomatoes, avocado, and herbs bursting with flavor and ready to be used in tasty recipes are certainly a cause for celebration. Heating the house with long oven baking is out of the question, and spending hours in the kitchen with a child is wonderful but not as important during this warm season as splashing in the pool or having fun outside.

Enjoy exploring these summer recipes. Do not hesitate to make substitutions when you see an ingredient at the market that looks ripe and luscious. Cold cherry soup could easily be cold peach soup, and zucchini and summer squash could replace cucumber in Persian *Mast o Khiar* to make it your own special yogurt dip.

Sometimes Rosh HaShanah is so early that it is officially in the summer, so think about the baking that could be done in advance to make your life easier as the calendar turns to fall.

Meggy Leves (Hungarian Cherry Soup)

Jews have lived in Hungary for over two thousand years, since the time of the Roman Empire—since before it was even Hungary!

Cherries are plentiful in Hungary, and cold cherry soup served as an appetizer before a meal is one of the most popular Hungarian soups for summer. In America, this soup is often a little bit sweeter, and people prefer to have it for dessert. Cherries are harvested between the end of May and August, but in Israel they are at their best and most plentiful just around the time of Shavuot. Served with sour cream, this soup is one of the traditional dishes to serve for the holiday.

Instead of using butter or oil with flour to thicken a recipe, Hungarian cooks use a mixture of sour cream, sugar, and flour, called a habaras, to thicken their sauces and soups.

16-ounce bag frozen tart or sweet
   cherries with juice
8 whole cloves
2 cinnamon sticks
Grated zest of ½ medium lemon
¼ cup sugar
3 cups water
½ cup dry red wine (Zinfandel or Shiraz
   would be good) or orange juice
1 teaspoon almond extract
Kosher salt, as needed

Habaras (thickening mixture):

¾ cup sour cream or Greek yogurt
2 tablespoons or more confectioners
   sugar, to taste
1 tablespoon all-purpose flour

1. Combine the first seven ingredients in a 3-quart saucepan. Bring to a boil and then simmer for 10 minutes, until cherries are tender and flavors have combined.

2. Remove 6 cherries to decorate the finished soup. Set aside. Discard cinnamon sticks and whole cloves.

3. Pass the cherries and liquid through a food mill to puree. Alternatively, blend the mixture in a blender until fairly smooth. Return the pureed soup to the pan. Add the almond extract and a pinch of salt. Reheat the soup on low heat while you make the *habaras*.

4. In a 1-quart bowl, using a whisk, whisk the sour cream, confectioners' sugar, and flour together.

5. Whisk some of the hot soup into the sour cream mixture, and then add all of the mixture back into the pot of soup. Simmer the soup, whisking constantly, for 3 minutes or until thickened.

6. Cover the surface of the soup with plastic wrap to prevent a tough skin from forming on the top, and chill. When ready to serve, spoon the soup into bowls and garnish with reserved cherries.

YIELD: 6 SERVINGS

Kitchen Conversations

Hungarian Jewish cooks who left Hungary before World War II brought many traditional Jewish dishes to their new homes, but those who left after 1956 or later don't know many of the traditional dishes. Why do you think that is so?

TINA'S TIDBITS

- *If you have the time, a cherry pitter, and an older child, you could make this soup with fresh cherries. However, most children under the age of ten will lose interest before all the cherries are pitted.*
- *This soup's flavor can be adjusted to a child's palate by adding a little more sugar if necessary.*
- *Sour cherries (the traditional type for this recipe) are very hard to find. However, the frozen sweet variety is not that sweet and will work in any recipe calling for tart cherries.*
- *Habaras is a traditional mixture that is used for thickening soups. The flour may be eliminated if you can't eat gluten. Just add a few more tablespoons of confectioners' sugar, which helps thicken the soup as well because it contains 3 percent cornstarch.*

Mast o Khiar (Persian Cucumber Yogurt Salad)

No one knows when yogurt was first discovered or created, but legend has it that thousands of years ago, a nomad traveling with milk in his goatskin sack found the milk slightly soured and thickened. He drank it and did not get sick, and its popularity was sealed for all time.

Yogurt, or mast as it is called in Persia (Iran), provides a cooling base for many salads and drinks for the hot summer months. During Shavuot, which falls in late May or June when weather in the Middle East becomes quite warm, dairy-based foods are traditionally served. The association between the holiday and dairy food has been linked to the giving of the laws of kashrut at Mount Sinai, when no properly slaughtered meat was available. It also probably didn't hurt that all the newborn lambs, goats, and cows in late spring meant milk was abundant.

The use of rose petals and rose water for flavoring was popular all over the Middle East and spread to Europe during the Middle Ages. Rose water fell out of favor in Europe once vanilla was introduced following the Spanish conquest of Mexico and Central America. Rose water always maintained its prominence in Sephardic cooking.

According to food historian Gil Marks, rosewater is a traditional flavoring for foods during Shavuot, which Sephardim call the "Feast of the Roses."

1. Place the yogurt in a 2-quart bowl. Stir with a rubber spatula so that the yogurt is smooth.

2. Add the remaining ingredients (except garnishes) and stir together.

3. Cover the bowl with plastic wrap, and refrigerate for at least one hour or preferably overnight to allow the flavors to blend.

4. Just before serving, stir the mixture and then spoon it into a serving dish. Sprinkle the top with some additional rose petals and chopped walnuts if desired.

5. Serve with soft Middle Eastern bread. This recipe can easily be doubled.

YIELD: 4–6 SERVINGS

1 cup thick Greek yogurt, preferably whole or 2%

¼ cup toasted walnuts, finely chopped

¼ cup golden raisins, coarsely chopped

½ cucumber cut into ¼-inch dice (approximately ¾ cup)

2 tablespoons fresh mint, finely minced

2 tablespoons fresh dill, finely minced

2 tablespoons fresh chives, finely minced

2 tablespoons fresh basil, finely minced

2 tablespoons dried rose petals, crushed or minced

1 clove garlic, finely minced

Salt and pepper to taste

Whole dried rose petals for garnish (optional)

1 tablespoon finely chopped walnuts for garnish (optional)

Kitchen Conversations

- Using your favorite herbs, fruits, vegetables, or spices, create your own special Shavuot dip!

- Persian cooking is very colorful. Point out all the different colors in this recipe or in the recipe you created.

TINA'S TIDBITS

- *If you can't find rose petals, substitute a few drops of rose water—you will be glad you did!*
- *Don't use dark raisins; the flavor isn't as good as the golden ones for this dish, and they turn the mixture light brown.*

Kale, Mango, and Almond Salad with Honey Ginger Dressing

Kale is a member of the cruciferous vegetable family and is a relative of broccoli, cabbage, cauliflower, and bok choy. It is grown in Israel and has become very popular because scientists have discovered its importance in promoting good health.

The mango tree is a distant relative of the cashew and pistachio trees, and its origins lie in southern India. Today there are hundreds of mango varieties in the world. Shelly, Omer, and the very popular Maya mango were developed in Israel over sixty years ago.

Almonds are one of the seven species of plants mentioned in the Bible that have always been associated with the Land of Israel. Together these foods create a terrific salad for a hot summer day, enjoyed with a slightly sweet salad dressing that complements the flavors.

1 pound fresh kale or 10 ounces baby kale

1 mango

⅓ cup dried sweetened cranberries or cherries

1 ounce candied ginger, about ¼ cup slivered (optional)

½ cup slivered almonds, roasted

Honey Ginger Dressing:

½ cup prepared mayonnaise

2 tablespoons wildflower or clover honey

2 tablespoons rice wine vinegar or any light fruit vinegar (e.g., apple cider vinegar, pear vinegar)

1 tablespoon canola oil or corn oil

½ teaspoon powdered ginger

1. If using whole kale leaves, pull the leaves off of the stems, and then layer the leaves on a cutting board. Using a chef's knife, cut thin strips of kale, and place them in a 4-quart mixing bowl. You should have about 12 cups.

2. Carefully cut the mango in half using a 5-inch utility knife or a special mango cutter. Remove the peel, and cut the mango into ½-inch cubes. Add the mango to the kale.

3. If using the candied ginger, carefully cut the chunks into slices and then into thin sticks using a paring knife. Add to the kale mixture. Add the roasted almonds, and then refrigerate the salad until ready to serve.

4. To make the dressing, place the mayonnaise in a 1-quart mixing bowl. Using a bar whisk, whisk the mayonnaise until it is smooth.

5. Add the remaining dressing ingredients to the mayonnaise, and whisk until smooth. Refrigerate until ready to use.

6. When ready to serve, toss the salad with enough dressing to coat all of the ingredients but not make it soupy.

YIELD: 6 SERVINGS

TINA'S TIDBITS

• *Although most children can tear the leaves of kale off of the thick stems, consider buying a 10-ounce bag of baby kale or kale-spinach mix if you are making this salad with a very young child.*

• *Layering the leaves of kale will save a great deal of time when cutting the kale into strips, but care should be taken when slicing, as the leaves do not lie flat on the cutting board.*

• *The candied ginger adds a wonderful taste to this salad. Rather than eliminating this ingredient because the child is too young to safely cut the ginger into thin strips, an adult should cut the ginger prior to making the salad.*

Kitchen Conversations

● There is an ethical concern today that food should be made from wholesome ingredients, farmers should be encouraged to grow a wide variety of crops, and people should support these farmers by eating the foods grown close to where they are grown. This helps sustain the crops and diminishes the amount of pollution created by the trucks delivering the produce. Is this ethical behavior new to the Jewish people? How has the Bible taught us to preserve and respect the crops in the field?

● During the summer, many fruits and vegetables are sold in local farmers' markets. Do you have a farmers' market in your area? Why not take a visit to one and buy some greens, fruits, and vegetables that are growing right now and create your own variation of this salad recipe?

Chicken Salad Veronique with Avocados

*A*lthough the first avocado tree was brought to Israel in 1908, avocados weren't grown on farms until the 1950s. Today there are over 3 million avocado trees growing all over Israel, mostly in the central coastal regions near Acre. Avocados are available almost all year round.

Israel's wine-making history goes back to biblical times. However, most of the grape varieties grown on the land before the late 1800s (when Baron Rothschild tried to renew the wine industry) were eating grapes brought to Palestine when the Ottomans ruled for four hundred years.

Using Israel's summer bounty, this recipe is a snap, especially if you have a deli cut the meat on its slicer into ½-inch-thick slices (#35 on some slicers). The name "Veronique" in French recipes signifies the inclusion of grapes.

---

8 ounces purchased deli chicken, cut into ½-inch-thick slices

1 ripe avocado

Juice of 1 lime

2 cups red or green seedless grapes

1 cup mayonnaise or to taste

2 tablespoons ketchup

1 good pinch of dried basil or summer savory

1–2 tablespoons sweet vermouth or apple juice

½ ripe avocado, sliced, for garnish (optional)

Toasted sliced almonds, for garnish (optional)

---

1. Using a large chef's knife, cut the chicken into ½-inch strips, and then cut the strips into ½-inch cubes. Place in a 2-quart bowl.

2. Cut 1 avocado into ½-inch cubes, and place in a 1-quart bowl with the lime juice. Toss using a rubber spatula.

3. Cut the grapes in half, add them to the chicken, and toss.

4. To prevent the mayonnaise from looking lumpy, first mix the mayonnaise in a 1-quart mixing bowl until it is smooth, and then combine it with the ketchup, dried herb, and sweet vermouth or apple juice and mix well.

5. Drain the avocado cubes. Using a rubber spatula, gently toss the avocados with the chicken and the grapes.

6. Add only enough of the mayonnaise mixture to moisten the salad. Mix carefully.

7. Thinly slice the remaining avocado half, if using, and coat with some additional lime juice. Arrange the slices over the top of the prepared salad, and sprinkle with some toasted almond slices if you want.

YIELD: 4 SERVINGS

Kitchen Conversations

● Discuss why avocado needs to be coated in lime juice. Is the avocado good if it does turn dark?

TINA'S TIDBITS

• *The easiest way to cut the meat is with the child's hand on top of the blade and the handle of the knife in his or her hand. Always remind the child to have his or her "fingers pointing up to the sky" so you can keep track of them!*

• *Buying thick slices of chicken make this a very easy dish to create. You can also use smoked turkey for added flavor. However, if you have chicken left over from soup, you can cut it into irregular chunks and use that instead.*

• *Never use light or fat free mayonnaise in a sauce, as the cellulose in the preparation will suck up any moisture from the sauce and make the salad dry and clumped together. Cutting fat? Then just use less.*

Greek Orzo Salad

R omaniotes are Greek Jews whose ancestors lived in Greece possibly as far back as the time of the Babylonian exile in 587 BCE. Oral tradition in that community teaches that Romaniotes have lived in Greece since the destruction of the second Temple in Jerusalem in 70 CE. The Jews of Greece suffered greatly during the Holocaust, and after the war many survivors moved to Israel or North America. Today there are only about 6000 Jews—including Romaniotes, Sephardim, and Ashkenazim—living in Greece.

Orzo is small barley-shaped pasta that is often found in Greek dishes. It's a perfect shape for this salad. Although spirals or macaroni can be used to make this dish, it will look more elegant using orzo.

1 cup orzo	2 lemons
2 medium tomatoes	⅓ cup extra virgin olive oil
⅓ cup fresh parsley	Kosher salt and freshly ground black
⅓ cup fresh basil	pepper to taste
½ cup crumbled feta cheese	

1. Cook the orzo in a large 4 quart pot for 10 minutes or until al dente (cooked through but not mushy). Drain in a colander and rinse under cold water. Drain again and place in a large mixing bowl.

2. Seed the tomatoes and then, using a sharp paring knife, cut the tomatoes into ¼ inch cubes. Add to the orzo.

3. Mince the parsley and the basil using a chef's knife and add to the orzo.

4. Add the feta cheese to the bowl.

5. Squeeze lemon or press lemon halves into a reamer over a small bowl and twist to get ¼ cup of juice. Combine the lemon juice, olive oil, and salt and pepper in a screw top jar and shake to combine.

6. Toss orzo mixture with just enough dressing to moisten but not to be too wet. Set aside remainder of the dressing Chill for at least half an hour. If needed, add a little more dressing to moisten the salad before serving.

SERVES 6-8

Kitchen Conversations:

● Before World War II the two largest Jewish communities in Greece were located in Athens and Thessaloniki. After the war many survivors left Greece. Today only 3,000 Jews live in Athens, 1,300 live in Thessaloniki, and 150 live in Chalkis – the oldest Jewish community in Europe. There are 50–150 Jews living in communities in Corfu, Ionnina, and Rhodes, which once were major Jewish centers. Look at a map of Greece and locate these cities. Why do you think Jews settled in those parts of Greece?

TINA'S TIDBITS

● *The inside of a tomato is soft and slippery but the skin is tough. A serrated knife is ideal because it cuts through the skin easily without destroying the tomato. After cutting a tomato in half, slice or dice the tomato, cutting through the meat of the tomato first, not the skin. This will avoid a slip of the knife and any accidental cuts of the fingers.*

● *The worst knife to give a child is a serrated plastic knife. These knives don't cut well, can slip, and the serrated edge can create a cut that doesn't heal smoothly.*

● *Rocking a chef's knife back and forth is the easiest, fastest, and safest way for a child to mince an herb.*

Nancy's Fresh Corn Salad

his recipe isn't necessarily Jewish, unless you consider that my rabbi, Nancy Kasten, served this simple but delicious salad at a Shabbat summer s'udah *(meal), a* s'udahsh'lishit—*or third meal—for Shabbat, under the rustling leaves of the trees beside a lake! According to the Talmud (Shabbat 117b), one is required to eat three meals over the course of Shabbat: one on Friday night, and two on Saturday. This, the Talmud teaches, is because God gave the Israelites in the desert an extra portion of manna for the Sabbath, but the verses describing this mention the word "to eat" three times.*

2 ears of corn with husk	1 tablespoon extra virgin olive oil
1 teaspoon Dijon mustard or to taste	Kosher salt and freshly ground black
1 tablespoon finely minced fresh dill	pepper to taste

1. Leave the husk on the corn, but cut 1 inch off of each end. Cook the corn in a microwave oven on high for 3 minutes. When it is cool enough to handle, remove the husk and silk.

2. Cut the corn off the cob using a paring knife or a large chef's knife—whichever is more comfortable to hold. Hold the corn upright, laying the wide, flat end of the cob on a cutting board. Hold the knife at a slight angle to the cob and slice down, top to bottom, to release the kernels.

3. Combine the corn kernels with the remaining ingredients in a medium serving bowl and serve at room temperature or cold.

YIELD: 3-4 SERVINGS

- *You can double this recipe, but don't cook more than two ears of corn at a time in the microwave.*
- *The silk and husk come off much more easily after the corn is cooked, but you may remove it beforehand if you prefer. You can also grill the corn in its husk to give the salad a slight smoky taste.*
- *A six- or seven-year old may feel comfortable using a paring knife alone, but littler hands should use a large-blade chef's knife so that you can share the knife handle and keep track of fingers!*

Kitchen Conversations

- Although corn is grown in Israel today, its production is quite small compared to other field crops like barley and wheat. Why do you think this is the case? Most of Israel is desert, and water is mainly found in the north of Israel.

- Since the late nineteenth century, Israel's land has been irrigated with water from the Sea of Galilee. Find pictures of Israel before 1900 and now. Discuss how the land could become so green and fertile.

- Discuss drip irrigation. If you have a straw, punch some holes over its length and fill it with water. Watch the water slowly drip to emphasize the importance of drip irrigation in growing crops.

Corn Pudding

Christopher Columbus discovered maize ("corn" was a generic word for grain in many European languages; maize eventually became known as "Indian corn" in Europe and simply "corn" in North America) when he landed in the New World in 1492. By 1500, maize was being grown in Spain. Shortly after that, Italians started growing it in Northern Italy, where the maize was most often made into a form of porridge or firm block of grain called polenta. Maize's popularity spread north and east to Romania, Slovenia, Serbia, and Bulgaria. The poor peasants of Romania ate so much of the cheap, plentiful grain that mamaliga, the name of their version of corn porridge, became a nickname for Romanian Jews.

Eventually maize was eaten all over Europe, but even as late as 1846 it did not appear in the English cookbook The Jewish Manual or Practical Information in Jewish and Modern Cookery by Lady Judith Cohen Montefiore. Lady Montefiore was the wife of the famous Jewish philanthropist Moses Montefiore. Hers was the first English-language Jewish cookbook ever printed. All the recipes in the book were popular recipes of the day adapted to use kosher ingredients. Although corn is kosher, it was rarely eaten in those days. Today corn is very popular, and this recipe is a delicious way to serve the sweet corn of summer.

3 tablespoons flour
¼ cup sugar
12-ounce can of vacuum packed corn (a short can containing very little liquid)
½ cup milk or soy creamer

2 large eggs
1 tablespoon vanilla
½ stick unsalted butter or pareve margarine, melted

1. Combine the flour, sugar, and corn in a 3-quart bowl.

2. Measure the ½ cup milk in a 2-cup liquid measuring cup. Add the eggs to the milk and mix with a fork to combine. Add to the corn, along with the vanilla and the melted butter. Make sure to stir the mixture while you add the hot melted butter.

3. Pour into a casserole and bake at 425°F for 35 minutes or until golden and a knife inserted into the center comes out moist but clear.

NOTE: This recipe can be doubled or quadrupled, but figure on a little more baking time—up to 1 hour.

YIELD: 4 SERVINGS

- *Defrosted frozen corn or even fresh corn can be used for this recipe, but canned corn is the most reliably sweet because it is processed shortly after picking.*

- *Melting butter in a mug or glass measuring cup with a handle will give an older child something to hold on to when removing the hot butter from the microwave. Make sure that the mug's handle doesn't heat up in the microwave. Some mugs' handles become as hot as the liquid they contain.*

- *If children are old enough to read, they are old enough to make this recipe with little supervision, but make sure an adult removes the casserole from the oven.*

- *Unless you are making this for a small dinner, double the recipe—it is that good!*

Kitchen Conversations

● Why would an immigrant continue to make foods from home? Why would an immigrant never make childhood dishes again?

● What's your favorite way to eat corn?

Green Tea–Jasmine Sorbet with Assorted Fruits

People are often surprised to learn that Jews have lived in eastern and southern Asia for over one thousand years! Jewish traders called Radanites, which in Persian means "one who knows the way," traveled on land and water routes that would bring them all the way to China. Radanites brought furs, swords, and other goods from Europe to China and returned with cinnamon, spices, and silk.

In Thailand, jasmine oil is often drizzled onto fresh fruit salad. In Iraq and Iran, orange blossom water often flavors sweets and fruit dishes. Using either flavoring will bring an exotic flavor to a modern dessert.

1 cup sugar
1 cup water
2–3 drops jasmine oil or 1 teaspoon
   orange blossom water
2½ cups water
2 jasmine or other floral green tea bags

3 cups assorted fruits such as
   cantaloupe, honeydew, pineapple,
   papaya, or mango, cut into 1-inch
   pieces
Canned *rambutan* or *longan* fruit,
   drained (optional)
Coconut milk (optional)

1. Place the sugar and 1 cup water in a 1-quart saucepan and bring to a boil. Boil over medium high heat for 15 minutes or until bubbles are large and begin to move slowly.

2. Remove from the heat, add the jasmine oil or orange blossom water, and transfer the mixture to a screw-top jar. Place the jar in the refrigerator or freezer to chill. Do not allow the mixture to freeze.

3. Meanwhile, measure the remaining water into a 4-cup glass measuring cup and microwave for 3 minutes. Place the two tea bags in the water, and set aside for 10 minutes.

4. Remove the tea bags and squeeze dry. Chill the tea in the refrigerator or freezer until ready to make the sorbet. Do not allow the mixture to freeze.

5. Combine the prepared cold tea with ¾ cup of the cold sugar syrup. Add more of the syrup if you want the sorbet to be sweeter.

6. Place the tea mixture in the container of an ice-cream maker and follow the manufacturer's instructions for making the sorbet. If you don't have an ice-cream maker, freeze the mixture in a pie plate or 8-inch square pan. Just before the sorbet is completely frozen, use a fork to scrape the sorbet into a bowl and freeze immediately. This is called a granita.

7. To serve, place some of the fruit in individual serving dishes, and place a scoop or two of the sorbet at the side. If you want, pour a little coconut milk over the fruit, like the Thais do.

- *This recipe is great to make with children who have short attention spans because it can be made in stages. Once you make the simple syrup (boiled water and sugar), it stays fresh in the refrigerator for months and will be available for the next time you want to make another sorbet.*

- *Of course, take care when making the syrup, as it is very hot and children are always curious to taste something sweet.*

- *Green tea contains caffeine. You might need to use a decaffeinated tea or a fruit herbal tea as an alternative.*

- *Consider using 2½ cups fruit juice instead of tea. You could also combine a banana with the juice in a blender, and then add the syrup and freeze.*

- Rambutan *and* longan *are fruits from Thailand that add an exotic touch to the salad. They come in cans and are found in Asian markets and some large-chain supermarkets. Children like the flavor.*

Kitchen Conversations

● Explore the different fruits that are available during the summer. Pick at least one you've never eaten before and try it. If possible, try a *rambutan*. It is absolutely beautiful, but I would stick to eating the canned version, as it is easier to prepare.

● Look for a map of the Far East in a book or on the Internet. Discuss how far the Radanites had to travel. What ways did they travel? On foot? On an animal? What type of animal?

Classic New York Egg Cream

An egg cream does not contain eggs or cream, just three basic ingredients. But an authentic New York egg cream must use Fox's U-Bet. Herman Fox, the Jewish grandfather of the present owner, founded a chocolate syrup company in New York sometime before the First World War. After the war, he decided to go to Texas and drill for oil. Down in Texas, the oilmen would say, "You bet," as a friendly way to talk to people. When the grandfather returned from Texas, he said, "I came back broke but with a good name for the syrup."

2 tablespoons chocolate syrup, homemade (next page) or Fox's U-Bet

⅓ cup milk
½ cup seltzer, plus more to top

1. Measure the syrup and milk into a 10-ounce tall glass.

2. Place a long, iced tea or soup spoon in the glass. Do not stir.

3. Pour the seltzer into the glass, stirring only at the bottom of the glass to mix the milk and syrup. The seltzer will blend in, and a creamy foam will form on the top. If you want, a little more seltzer can be added.

YIELD: 1 SERVING

Homemade Chocolate Syrup

¼ **cup unsweetened Dutch processed cocoa**

1 cup sugar

Pinch of salt

½ **cup water**

½ **teaspoon vanilla**

1. Whisk the cocoa, sugar, and salt together in a 1½-quart saucepan. Add the water slowly to the pan as you whisk to dissolve the sugar and cocoa and to prevent lumps.

2. Bring the mixture to a boil, and then reduce the heat to medium.

3. Simmer for three minutes, stirring occasionally with the whisk. The mixture should be slightly reduced and appear thicker.

4. Remove from heat and whisk in the vanilla. Pour into a clean jar, cover, and refrigerate until ready to use.

YIELD: 1 CUP OF SYRUP

Kitchen Conversations

Look at a picture of an old seltzer bottle. Have you ever seen one? Has your grandparent or parent ever seen one? Talk about the foods that were easily available fifty years ago that are rare to find now.

TINA'S TIDBITS

- *Unless the child is two or under, have the child hold the glass in one hand and the long spoon in another while an adult adds the seltzer. This helps develop gross motor coordination.*
- *Seltzer has no added salt (club soda does) and will create a bigger foam head on your glass.*

Part II

SHABBAT SPECIALTIES

CHALLAH FRENCH TOAST,
PAGE 86

Shabbat has always been important to the Jewish people, certainly from the time they were given the Ten Commandments and it was divined the holiest day of the week. Elevating Shabbat to a special day has long included creating a beautiful table for the Friday night meal, making the challah with fancy white milled flour, and serving a special meal to provide a warm environment for family and friends to congregate. Observance of Shabbat was so important that traders on long travels away from home would schedule their stops for Shabbat to coincide with a community that had a Jewish home. This practice often led to the trader putting down roots and starting a business in that community, and Jewish homesteads were created.

Today Shabbat often serves a similar function. Family and friends gather to celebrate the Sabbath and form tight communities. Sometimes Shabbat dinner is the preamble to a weekend with a visiting grandchild or young relative. What started as the end of the week begins a weekend of building memories through shared experiences. Cooking is one of those experiences that lasts a lifetime and gives a great opportunity to pass down family stories and traditions. You might not feel completely rested at the end of the weekend, but the peace of Shabbat and the pleasure of shared activity will renew you for the week to come.

Challah is an integral part of Shabbat observance, so I have included a number of recipes to excite your creativity. The leftovers can be transformed into additional recipes.

Because we are instructed to elevate the Sabbath in praise of God, communities all over the world seemed to gravitate to chicken as one of the major protein choices for the Sabbath meal. For poor Jews, chicken was likely the least expensive, most readily available meat. Even Jews who lived in areas that had access to an abundance of fish often chose chicken as the main component of their special meal (fish was always included in Sabbath and holiday meals, as it represented fertility, productivity, and success).

Kugel had its roots in the laws pertaining to cooking for Shabbat, but over the centuries it was created from many different ingredients. The story is told in the following pages.

Enjoy your Shabbat surrounded by those you hold dear, and create conversations and moments you will always remember.

Challah

Basic Easy Challah

*M*aking challah together is fun, creative, and rewarding and builds family memories for a lifetime. This recipe can be completed in three hours, with time in between for other activities. The dough can be prepared, put in the refrigerator to rise slowly, and then braided and baked just before Shabbat. Imagine the wonderful aroma in your kitchen! Do not be put off by the number of steps. I have described each step separately so that even an adult beginner cook can successfully make challah, with or without a child's help!

Here is the basic recipe, with variations listed below.

7 cups bread flour	¾ cup sugar
2 packets rapid rise yeast	1 tablespoon corn oil (or other
1 tablespoon kosher salt	vegetable oil), for greasing the bowl
4 large eggs	Egg wash: 1 egg mixed with
1 cup corn oil (or other vegetable oil)	1 tablespoon water and 1 teaspoon
1½ cups water	honey

1. Place the bread flour, yeast, and salt in the bowl of an electric mixer fitted with a dough hook. Mix on low speed (#1) for 10 seconds to combine.

2. Lightly beat the eggs with a fork in a 1-quart bowl until combined. Set aside.

3. Measure the oil in a 1-cup liquid measuring cup. Set aside.

4. Measure the 1½ cups water in a 2-cup glass measuring cup. Add the sugar and stir once or twice. Microwave the water/sugar on high for **exactly** 1 minute 20 seconds.

5. With the mixer on low speed (#1), immediately add the hot water/sugar mixture straight from the microwave; then add the eggs and then the oil.

6. With the mixer on medium speed (#2), continue mixing with the dough hook for 6 minutes. If the dough is too sticky, add as much as an additional ½ cup flour until a floured finger poked into the dough does not stick to the dough.

7. If using additional ingredients (see Challah Your Way!, Page 80), add them to the bread dough now.

8. Mix on medium speed (#2) for another 3 minutes. The mixture should be satiny smooth.

9. Grease a 4-quart bowl with 1 tablespoon oil. Add the dough to the bowl, turning the dough over to coat it on all sides. Cover the bowl with plastic wrap, and let the dough rise in a draft-free spot until doubled in size, about 1½ hours. (I like to use an out-of-the-way corner in my kitchen or a warming drawer set on low.)

10. When the dough is ready, remove it from the bowl, punch it gently with your fist, and cut into 4 pieces.

11. Shape the dough into loaves or braided loaves. Line 2 cookie sheets with parchment paper, and place 2 formed breads on each. Let rise until doubled (about 45 minutes).

12. Preheat the oven to 325°F. For even baking, use two ovens if possible, one cookie sheet per oven.

13. Mix the egg wash ingredients together in a small glass bowl with a fork or bar whisk. Using a pastry brush, brush the tops of the loaves with the egg wash, and place the cookie sheets on the lower racks of two ovens or on two racks of one oven positioned such that one sheet is on the left and the other on the right, allowing air to circulate inside the oven.

14. As soon as you place the loaves in the oven, turn up the temperature to 350°F. Bake the loaves for 25 minutes or until the loaves are golden brown and have a hollow sound when tapped. Cool completely before slicing.

YIELD: 4 LOAVES

TINA'S TIDBITS

• *It is important to add the ingredients in the order listed because adding the water to the flour before the oil allows the gluten to develop better and gives you a lighter loaf.*

• *Measuring ingredients is a great way to reinforce numbers with young children and fractions with older children. It can also enhance their gross motor coordination, requiring the use of two hands at one time.*

• *Before you attempt to check to see if the dough is the right consistency,* **turn the mixer off!** *Children should be told to wait until you have turned the machine off or unplugged it before they check the dough so that they don't accidentally get their fingers caught.*

Challah Your Way!

Make this recipe your own and start your own family tradition. Here are a few suggested additions to step 7:

- Add 2 tablespoons poppy seeds to the flour and 1 cup of dark raisins.

- Add ½ teaspoon cinnamon to the flour and 1 cup finely chopped apples.

- Add 1 teaspoon vanilla with the eggs and 1 cup chocolate chips.

- Add the grated zest of 1 orange to the flour, substitute ¼ cup orange juice for ¼ cupof the water, and add 1 cup dried cranberries or cherries.

TINA'S TIDBITS

- *To make sure the dough isn't too moist, dip your finger in some flour, and then poke the dough. If your finger doesn't stick, then the dough is perfect! If the dough is too sticky, place an extra ¼ cup of flour on a board, and knead the dough by hand until it feels satiny smooth. Don't add too much flour or the finished bread will be tough and dry.*
- *Although microwaves seem safe because they don't get hot, their contents do. An adult or older child should be the one to remove food from the microwave, especially if the unit is at eye level or higher.*

Kitchen Conversations

- Why do we braid challah? Why do we make 6 braids?

- Why is challah shaped in a spiral or round loaf for Rosh HaShanah?

Round Algerian Challah

*J*ews have lived in Algeria for twenty-five hundred years! Jews once lived in all the countries around the Mediterranean Sea. When the Moors conquered the region in the late seventh century, most of the time Jews were allowed to live freely and succeed in commerce and trade. However, the quality of Jewish life in Algeria changed drastically once Israel was declared a state and Algeria gained its independence from France. It was no longer safe to live there. Many Algerian Jews emigrated to France, Israel, or the United States. In 1948, 140,000 Jews lived in Algeria. Today there are fewer than 100.

Shaped in a loaf, a braid, or a round spiral, this challah is delicious all year long. There are no eggs used in this dough, and the egg wash can be eliminated to produce a loaf of bread that is egg-free for those who are allergic to eggs. Check out the suggestion for spiced apple stuffing for the bread, a great addition to your Shabbat or Rosh HaShanah meal!

---

8 cups bread flour, divided
2 packages rapid rise yeast
1½ teaspoons kosher salt
2 cups water
¾ cup corn oil
2 tablespoons sugar

Zest of ½ medium orange, finely grated
  or chopped
1½ teaspoons orange blossom water
Egg wash: 1 egg mixed with 1 teaspoon
  water (optional)
¼ cup sesame seeds

---

1. Combine 7 cups of the flour, the yeast, and the salt in the large bowl of an electric mixer fitted with a dough hook.

2. Place the water, oil, sugar, and orange zest in a 4-cup glass measuring cup, and microwave for 1½ minutes. Stir to dissolve the sugar, and then microwave on high for another 30 seconds until the water is very warm (130°F). Remove from the microwave, and add the orange blossom water.

3. With the mixer on medium speed (#2), **immediately** add the warm water/oil mixture to the mixing bowl. If necessary, stop the mixer after a minute and scrape down the sides of the bowl with a rubber spatula to incorporate all the flour.

4. Gradually add some of the remaining flour to the bowl and keep mixing for another 7 minutes until the dough is satiny smooth. If you want, you can knead the dough by hand for 7–10 minutes on a lightly floured surface until enough of the flour is incorporated and the dough is satiny smooth. Oiling your hands might help when kneading the dough.

5. Turn your oven on for **1 minute** (doesn't matter what temperature as it will barely heat.) **Turn the oven off!**

6. Oil a 4-quart bowl, and place the dough in the bowl, turning the dough around once to coat it with oil. Cover with plastic wrap. Place the bowl of dough in the **turned-off** (but slightly warm) oven. Let the dough rise for 1½ hours or until the dough has risen to the top of the bowl. If you have a warming drawer, turn it on to the lowest setting and let the dough rise there.

7. When the dough has risen, remove the plastic wrap, punch down the dough, and

place on a flat surface. Cut the dough into 4 equal pieces.

8. Shape each piece into a rope about 2 inches thick and 12 inches long. Coil the dough around itself and tuck the end under to make a large, slightly domed spiral of dough. Line 2 cookie sheets with parchment paper, place 2 loaves on each, and return to the turned-off oven. Let the dough rise for 45 minutes to an hour.

9. Remove the loaves of bread from the oven.

10. Preheat oven to 350°F. Make sure you place the racks so that there is enough room for the loaves on the bottom to rise.

11. If using the egg wash, beat the egg in a small glass dish with 1 teaspoon water. Brush this egg wash over the bread, and then sprinkle each loaf with 1 tablespoon sesame seeds.

12. Bake for 25 minutes or until the bread sounds hollow when tapped with your finger. Remove from the oven and immediately cover with a kitchen towel to keep moist. When cool, wrap tightly with plastic wrap or foil.

YIELD: 4 LOAVES

Kitchen Conversations

● Breads in the Maghreb (North Africa) are often shaped into spirals. Jews in Algeria often shape a bird out of the dough or place a dough bird on top of the loaf to symbolize our wishes going to heaven. How else could you shape the dough for Rosh HaShanah?

TINA'S TIDBITS

- *The water should be hot when you dip a finger into the mixture but not hot enough to burn. It is best to use a thermometer if you have one, especially if cooking with a very young child.*
- *Children can use the microwave if it is low enough for them to peer into it.*
- *If you truly need to make this bread egg free, mix 1 teaspoon honey and 1 teaspoon oil into 2 tablespoons water and brush on top of the bread.*
- *Orange blossom water gives a subtle flavor to the bread. If you don't have it, add ½ teaspoon orange extract to the dough instead.*

Challah Cheese Soufflé

When the Jews left Egypt and wandered in the desert, God sent manna from the heavens to feed them. On Friday they received a double portion because they could not work on the Sabbath. That is why we have the tradition of two loaves of challah on our Shabbat tables. Dew fell from heaven to protect the manna, and that is why many Jews today either cover their challahs with a special cloth or sprinkle sesame seeds on top to symbolize the dew.

Unless you have a large family or your two challahs are very small, you will have a lot of challah left over! This recipe and the two others that follow are good ways to use these leftovers. Not only do the recipes provide delicious ways to engage a child in the kitchen, they offer opportunities to discuss the meaning of Shabbat and its customs.

A modern version of a soufflé, this recipe will not fail or collapse, since bread binds the ingredients together. This dish is perfect for younger children with short attention spans because the dish needs to be assembled several hours ahead of time or even the night before. This gives the challah time to absorb the liquids, and the dish will puff up when baked.

1–1½ medium challahs (approximately 12 cups of challah cubes)
1 stick unsalted butter
6 eggs
2 cups milk (whole, 1% or 2 %)
1 teaspoon salt
10 grindings of freshly ground black pepper

⅛ teaspoon nutmeg
12–16 ounces shredded sharp cheddar cheese or Jarlsberg cheese (about 3½ cups grated)
Additional butter or cooking spray for greasing the pan

1. Cut challah into ½-inch slices, and then cut the slices into ½-inch cubes; or pull the bread apart into small pieces if that is easier. The crust does not need to be removed if it isn't hard. Set aside.

2. In a 1-quart glass bowl covered with a sheet of paper towel, melt the butter in the microwave according to the manufacturer's setting. Set aside.

3. Using a medium whisk, whisk the eggs and the milk together with the salt, pepper, and nutmeg in a 2-quart mixing bowl. Add the melted butter and whisk to combine. Set aside.

4. If not using packaged shredded cheese, grate the cheese on a coarse grater.

5. Grease a 2-quart casserole or soufflé dish with butter or nonstick cooking spray.

6. Arrange ⅓ of the bread cubes in the bottom of the pan, and then layer ⅓ of the cheese on top. Make 2 more layers of bread and cheese, and then pour the egg/milk mixture over all. Lightly press down to make sure all of the bread layers are covered with liquid ingredients.

7. Cover the dish with plastic wrap, and refrigerate for at least 4 hours or overnight.

8. When ready to cook, preheat the oven to 350°F. Bake the dish in the center of the oven for 45 minutes to 1 hour or until the top is golden brown and a thin pointy knife inserted in the center comes out wet but clear.

YIELD: 6 SERVINGS

Kitchen Conversations

● Discuss why challah is so special for Shabbat. What's your favorite challah? Does it have raisins? Plain? Flavored? Whole wheat?

● Did Jews always eat fancy braided bread?

TINA'S TIDBITS

• *Older children will enjoy the reinforcement of their math and geometry lessons with this recipe, and younger children can easily make this dish if you let them break the challah into little pieces with their hands and you buy packaged shredded cheese.*

• *Butter often splatters when melting because it naturally contains some water. To avoid having it explode all over your microwave oven, cover the dish lightly with a piece of paper towel when melting.*

• *It goes without saying that children under the age of ten or those not tall enough to reach into an oven should not be removing any hot baking dish from an oven.*

• *If a child is doing the testing to see if the soufflé is fully baked (step 8), the test should be done out of the oven with the soufflé dish placed on a counter. If the soufflé is not ready and it is taken out of the oven for too long, it will become dense when fully baked, so young children should not do the testing.*

Challah French Toast

T his recipe takes basic French toast to new heights! If you start out with rich challah bread, how can you go wrong? Children of all ages like to make French toast. It requires few utensils and short attention spans are no problem!

I use ice cream in this recipe because it is more likely that you have a container of ice cream in the house than a container of heavy cream or even half-and-half. And, of course, children think it's fun to have ice cream in their breakfast. This recipe can easily be made with milk and can certainly be doubled, which is not a bad idea if you want to serve more than two people and your challah is homemade (it will absorb more of the custard mixture).

Here is another way to extend the joy of Shabbat and its special bread. Enjoy!

---

1 egg

Pinch of kosher salt

1 cup premium vanilla ice cream, half-
   and-half, or milk

¼ cup light brown sugar

½ teaspoon cinnamon

½ teaspoon vanilla extract (omit if
   using ice cream)

Zest of ½ fresh orange

Challah bread, crust included

2 or more tablespoons unsalted butter

Pure maple syrup, confectioners' sugar,
   or fruit, if desired

---

1. Combine the egg and a pinch of salt with a fork in a 2-quart bowl.

2. Add the ice cream or milk, brown sugar, cinnamon, vanilla, and orange zest to the bowl, and whisk well to combine. Pour into a 9-inch pie plate or flat-bottomed bowl. Set aside while you prepare the bread.

3. Cut the bread into four ¾-inch slices. If desired, use a cookie cutter to cut designs from the center of the slices.

4. Place 2 bread slices or cutout shapes in the egg/cream mixture. Turn the slices over to absorb more egg mixture, but be careful that they don't absorb too much or they will fall apart when transferred to the frying pan.

5. Heat a 10-inch frying pan over medium heat for 15 seconds. Add 2 tablespoons butter to the frying pan, and swirl the pan around to melt the butter and coat the bottom of the pan.

6. Using a large metal turner, carefully lift the bread slices from the egg/cream mixture and place in the pan. Fry on one side until the bottom of the bread is golden brown, about 3 minutes. Turn the

slices over and continue cooking until the slices are soft but evenly golden.

7. Remove to a warm plate. Add more butter to pan, as needed, before you fry additional slices of soaked bread. Continue with more bread slices or shapes until all the egg/cream mixture is used.

8. Serve with maple syrup, confectioners' sugar, and/or fresh fruit, if desired.

YIELD: 2–4 SERVINGS, DEPENDING ON THE SIZE AND SHAPE OF THE BREAD

Kitchen Conversations

● Older children can create a design on paper, cut it out, and then use it as a template to cut the bread into a special shape with a sharp paring knife.

● *Hiddur mitzvah* means elevating a commandment by taking extra time to make it special as a way to honor God. Is challah different from the everyday bread Jews ate in Europe? How is this recipe a way to demonstrate hiddur mitzvah? What other ways can you add to your Shabbat or holiday observance?

TINA'S TIDBITS

• *All ages can make this, but very young children must be on a sturdy step stool that will bring the stove to their waist height. I like to hold the child by the waist with my left arm and then help him or her add the bread with my right.*

• *Two- to four-year-olds might be intimidated by the stove, so you might wind up doing all of the cooking. That's okay. They have helped with the preparation and will be satisfied.*

• *Using a rasp-type zester is very easy and requires little pressure on the peel of the orange, so little hands can do it. In addition, some zesters catch the zest so you don't have to scrape up the little pieces.*

Challah "Babka" Bread Pudding

Babka, or *"grandmother's cake," refers to the* babcia *(in Slavic languages) or* bubbe *(in Yiddish), so called because in the early 1800s this cake was made in a high fluted pan that looked like a grandmother's skirt.*

Babka is a traditional Polish/Ukrainian yeast cake that was originally made from rich challah dough rolled around a sweet cinnamon or fruit filling. Baked with the challah, it was a Friday afternoon treat for children waiting for Shabbat to arrive.

This recipe is a twist on classic babka. Instead of being made with challah dough, it is made from the baked challah! Chocolate and cinnamon flavor the pudding, and the classic streusel topping finishes off this wonderful treat.

One 1-pound challah (raisin or plain), preferably a few days old	4 eggs
8 ounces Israeli chocolate spread or chocolate-hazelnut spread	1½ teaspoons vanilla
1 stick unsalted butter or margarine	½ teaspoon cinnamon
¼ cup light brown sugar	2 cups milk (skim, 2%, or whole)
	Additional butter for greasing dish

Topping:

3 tablespoons unsalted butter, at room temperature or slightly softened in the microwave
½ cup flour
½ cup sugar
½ teaspoon vanilla

1. Butter a 2-quart oval or rectangular baking dish. Set aside.

2. Slice the challah into ¾-inch slices. Spread the chocolate filling over each slice of bread using a small bent spatula or utility knife. Arrange in the casserole to fit evenly.

3. Microwave the butter in a 2-quart glass bowl until melted. Add the brown sugar, and stir to dissolve.

4. Add the eggs, vanilla, cinnamon, and milk to the bowl, and whisk to combine well.

5. Carefully pour the egg/milk mixture over the bread slices. Using a wide metal spatula, gently press down on the bread slices to submerge them under the custard. Place a plate or bowl on top of the casserole to weight the challah down. Set aside on the counter for 30 minutes while you make the topping.

6. Preheat the oven to 350°F.

7. Place the topping ingredients in a 1-quart mixing bowl, and squeeze the mixture together using your hands at first and then fingertips, to evenly combine all ingredients and make a crumble.

8. Sprinkle the topping evenly over the bread/custard in the baking dish.

9. Bake for 35–45 minutes or until puffed and golden. Serve warm or at room temperature.

YIELD: 8–12 SERVINGS

Kitchen Conversations

- Does your family have a special dessert that you make for Shabbat or a holiday?

- Where did the recipe come from? Whose family? What country?

- Has the recipe changed over the years because of modern equipment?

TINA'S TIDBITS

- *The best knife for slicing bread is a serrated knife. However, if cut with a serrated knife the wound usually forms scar tissue. Therefore, with the exception of older children (7+) I would recommend pre-slicing the challah before you begin to make the recipe.*

CLASSIC JEWISH DELI
CHICKEN SALAD, PAGE 94

Chicken

Breaded Chicken Schnitzel

Schnitzel is a very popular preparation served on Shabbat around the world. Its origins are Austrian, and it refers to any meat, pounded thin, coated with some breading, and then pan-fried. The origin of this dish can, again, be traced back to the Arab influence on Jewish cooking in Spain (Jews coated fish with flour or breading and fried it in oil). Expelled Spanish Jews brought this technique to Northern Italy, where veal was substituted for the fish (food dipped in egg and then in seasoned bread crumbs always has the adjective "Milanese"). The Hapsburg Empire ruled Milan and Northern Italy from the early 1700s to the mid-1800s, and their chefs learned many cooking techniques from the Italians. This particular technique gained great favor in Vienna, and the breaded chop transformed into a flattened cutlet. Schnitzel in German means "cutlet," and so a culinary tradition was born.

1 pound boneless breast of chicken

¼ cup all-purpose flour (or matzah cake meal for Passover)

1 large egg

1 tablespoon water

1 cup panko bread crumbs or matzah meal

1 teaspoon salt

½ teaspoon ground black pepper (20 grindings in a pepper mill)

½ teaspoon garlic powder

2–4 tablespoons extra virgin olive oil

1. Remove the fillet from the chicken breast. Place the chicken breast smooth side down on a cutting board. Cover the chicken with a plastic storage bag, and using a meat mallet or a rolling pin, pound until the breast is about ¼-inch thick. If the pieces are large, cut them to be around 3–4 inches wide.

2. Place the flour (or matzah cake meal) on a plate. Set aside.

3. Mix the egg with the water in a shallow soup bowl. Set aside.

4. Combine the panko bread crumbs (or matzah meal) with the salt, pepper, and garlic powder on a plate. Set aside.

5. Coat the chicken with flour, dip in the egg, and then coat well with the seasoned crumbs.

6. Heat a 10-inch nonstick frying pan over high heat for 15 seconds. Add 2 tablespoons of olive oil and heat for another 10 seconds. Reduce the temperature to medium if the oil is smoking and too hot.

7. Place a few pieces of chicken in the pan. Cook for 2 minutes or until the underside is golden. Turn the chicken over using a turner or tongs, and continue to cook for another 2–3 minutes until golden.

NOTE: Serve plain or topped with Marinara sauce.

YIELD: 4 SERVINGS

Kitchen Conversations

● On a map, trace the route of the breaded cutlet from the Middle East to North Africa to Spain to Italy to Austria to Israel and North America.

● Do you know any other foods that have traveled so far? Pasta? Ice cream? Search the Internet for some clues.

TINA'S TIDBITS

• *Frying in olive oil serves two purposes, especially when cooking with children:*
  1. *It contains no water like margarine and therefore will not splatter.*
  2. *It has a higher smoking point than other oils typically used for frying, so meat can be cooked fast and bread crumbs won't burn in that short time.*
• *Chicken does not need to be tenderized, so do not use the spiked side of a meat mallet, especially with children.*
• *Old recipes called for waxed paper for pounding meat, but a plastic bag won't rip or embed particles of paper or plastic in your food.*
• *Another advantage of pounding the cutlets is that each cutlet can be cut in half or thirds or even in strips so that the portion size is appropriate for children.*

Classic Jewish Deli Chicken Salad

Our Jewish ancestors who lived in poor regions of Eastern Europe and Russia always had to be creative to feed their families. On Shabbat, when it was important to elevate the food and the table to make them special for the Sabbath, it was doubly important to make the most of the food, since the meal often used more expensive ingredients than were eaten during the rest of the week. A great example of this is the use of chicken on Shabbat. Every part of the chicken needed to be used to provide nutrition for the family. As a matter of fact, the classic Shabbat meal was a result of our ancestors' resourcefulness. From one chicken, you make soup, use the fat from the soup to spread on the challah, stuff the skin of the chicken (for a dish called helzel), and chop the liver. Of course, we cannot forget the meat of the chicken, which was eaten!

When immigrants came to North America, they still made chicken soup for Shabbat and holidays, but they often had a beef or veal dish as the main course. Then in 1905, Richard Hellmann, an immigrant from Germany, opened a deli on the Upper West Side of New York City. His wife, Nina, created a special mayonnaise sauce that he used in salads and on sandwiches that became so popular he began selling the sauce as "Hellmann's Best Mayonnaise." The rest is history, and New York–style delis all over the country wouldn't think of using anything but Hellmann's in their cooking, especially in chicken salad! And **the best** *chicken salad is made from the chicken cooked in the soup!*

1 cut-up whole chicken, cooked
  (preferably stewed for soup)
2 stalks of celery
3 or more carrots
1 tablespoon grated onion or more to
  your taste

Salt and pepper to taste
½–1 cup Hellmann's mayonnaise
1 can jellied cranberry sauce (optional)

1. Skin the chicken, and pull the meat off the bones.

2. Shred the chicken with your fingers to make sure no bone is present. Place the chicken in a 3-quart bowl.

3. Wash and then dice the celery, and add it to the chicken.

4. Peel the carrots, cut off the tips, and holding on to the big end, grate the carrots into the bowl with the chicken and the celery. Discard the top of the carrot.

5. Add the grated onion, salt, pepper, and mayonnaise, and mix with a fork or spoon until well blended and moistened. Use as much of the mayonnaise as needed to create the texture you want. Refrigerate until ready to serve.

6. For a fun and decorative way to serve the chicken salad, line a 2-quart bowl with plastic wrap and spoon the chicken mixture into it. Press down firmly on the chicken so that it will mold.

7. Meanwhile, slice the cranberry sauce into ½-inch slices. Using a small cookie cutter or sharp knife, make designs in the sauce slices.

8. To serve, turn the bowl with the chicken salad upside down onto a serving plate. Remove the bowl and wrap, and using a small spreader or the back of a spoon, coat with a thin layer of mayonnaise. Decorate the top and sides of the chicken salad with the cranberry sauce cutouts, and serve with crackers or rolls.

Kitchen Conversations

Baltashchit is the Jewish value of not being wasteful or unnecessarily destructive. Our ancestors practiced this law in their use of Shabbat chickens. What can you do to practice *baltashchit* to help protect our environment today?

TINA'S TIDBITS

* *This is a perfect recipe to make with children over the weekend after the Shabbat soup is cooked and you have that great chicken left over!*
* *To prepare the chicken, reheat it in the microwave just until warm. It shouldn't be hot. Warmed, the skin will slide off easily and the meat will separate from the bone with little effort.*
* *When spooning mayonnaise from the jar and adding it to the chicken, do not touch the chicken with that spoon and then put it back in the jar. The bacteria from the chicken will grow in the jar, and future use could make someone ill.*
* *If the children are young or if your only grater is one of those metal boxes with grates on each side, opt for using the grating disk on a food processor to save little knuckles from getting bruised.*
* *Plastic grating plates or rasp-type graters are my choices for safe utensils for children to use.*

Roasted Chicken South African Style

Portuguese Jewish mapmakers and scientists participated in the exploration of the Cape of Good Hope in 1497 (which also happened to be the year that the Inquisition came to Portugal and the Jews were expelled). When the Dutch East India Company founded Cape Town in 1652 to provide a place for their ships to trade in spices and other goods, Jews came to the region to set up markets for the merchants (although they were not allowed to be openly Jewish). When religious freedom was declared in 1806 by the British, twenty Jews came to South Africa from Germany and Holland to establish the vast network of trade, shipping, and fishing industries. When diamonds were discovered in 1867, this network helped Jews successfully get involved in diamond mining. The famous diamond company, DeBeers, was founded by two Jews, Sammy Marks and Barney Barnato. Mr. Marks went on to become South Africa's biggest industrialist and Jewish philanthropist.

Most of South Africa's Jews are Ashkenazic, coming to the region in the late 1800s from Lithuania to escape persecution and to achieve financial security. South Africa's doors were also open to Jewish immigrants between 1933 and 1935, but almost no Jews were allowed in during the Holocaust. Many Jews emigrated away from South Africa to Israel and North America during the 1970s because of the high crime rate and political unrest over apartheid (which most Jews did not support). The Ashkenazic influence in food choices is still present in the Jewish community living in South Africa today, and here is a dish that is often served on Shabbat.

4- to 5-pound whole chicken
1 teaspoon kosher salt
½ teaspoon ground ginger
½ teaspoon freshly ground black
  pepper
1 apple, Fuji, Gala, or Jonagold
1 medium onion
8 small red new potatoes, unpeeled

2 tablespoons rendered chicken fat or
  olive oil
1½ tablespoons grated, peeled, fresh
  gingerroot
1 tablespoon honey (optional)
⅓ cup apple juice
⅓ cup chicken broth or water

1. Rinse the chicken cavity well with running tap water, and place in a roasting pan large enough to hold the chicken with 1–2 inches open around the sides.

2. Place the salt, ground ginger, and black pepper in a small glass bowl and stir to combine.

3. Measure ½ teaspoon of this spice mixture and sprinkle it inside the cavity of the bird. Rub the spice mixture all over the inside of the chicken and set aside.

4. Core the apple, and cut into 16 pieces. There is no need to peel the apple. Peel the onion, and cut it into 16 pieces as well. Cut the potatoes into quarters.

5. Stuff as many pieces of apple and onion as you can into the cavity of the bird. Place any remaining pieces around the bird in the pan. Place the quartered potatoes around the bird as well.

6. Combine the chicken fat or olive oil with the remaining spices in the dish, along with the grated ginger and the honey (if using) until well mixed. Spread the seasoned fat all over the outside of the chicken, massaging the mixture well into the chicken skin.

7. Preheat the oven to 350°F. Cover the chicken with a tent of foil, making sure that the shiny side of the foil is facing you.

8. Pour the apple juice and chicken broth around the bird.

9. Roast the bird for 1 hour, and then remove the foil tent. Using a turkey baster, baste with some of the juices that have collected on the bottom of the pan.

10. Continue roasting the chicken until it is tender and the skin is golden brown.

11. Let the chicken sit for 10 minutes to reabsorb some of its juices. Carve and serve with the roasted vegetables and accumulated gravy.

YIELD: 4-6 SERVINGS

Kitchen Conversations

This recipe is similar to Shabbat chicken dishes made in homes all across North America, but it comes from a community thousands of miles away. If you visited the Jewish community in South Africa, what do you think would be familiar? What would be different? Why?

TINA'S TIDBITS

• *Children of all ages can prepare this recipe. However, first check the inside of the chicken to make sure there are no sharp edges from any broken bones, so no one gets cut.*

• *Children should not take the roasting pan out of the oven for basting.*

• *A young child can baste but will need your hand guiding him or her when filling the baster and squeezing the bulb, to prevent the hot liquid from unintentionally squirting out and burning someone.*

Supermarket Checkout Chicken

*S*ometimes we don't have a lot of time to cook or a lot of time to cook with a child. However, here's a dish that is delicious and quick and will introduce a young cook to a blend of flavors that is at once familiar and exotic. Served over pasta or couscous, this dish is sure to be a hit!

The spices and dried fruits in this recipe remind us of Jewish cooking on the spice route in the Middle East and the use of fruits in slow-cooked dishes in Jewish kitchens in Eastern Europe.

---

1 supermarket-prepared whole roasted chicken (about 3–4 pounds)

1 cup drippings from the roasted chicken container (or 1 cup concentrated canned chicken broth)

¾ cup concentrated canned chicken broth

½ cup orange juice

¼ teaspoon ground ginger

¼ teaspoon ground coriander

¾ teaspoon ground cinnamon

Salt and freshly ground black pepper to taste

½ tablespoon (1½ teaspoons) olive or vegetable oil

8 dried, pitted plums, cut in half

5 large medjool dates, pitted and cut into quarters

6 large dried apricots, cut into quarters

2 tablespoons golden raisins

2 tablespoons slivered almonds (optional)

---

1. Cut or pull the chicken pieces apart so that you have 8 pieces (2 pieces of white breast meat, 2 pieces of dark thigh meat, 2 legs, and 2 wings). If you prefer, you can pull all the skin and bones from the meat and shred the cooked chicken with your fingers into bite-sized pieces. Set the chicken aside while you prepare the sauce.

2. Combine the chicken drippings, broth, orange juice, and seasonings in a 1-quart measuring cup or bowl. Set aside.

3. Heat a 10-inch frying pan or 3-quart saucepan for 15 seconds. Add the oil and then heat for another 10 seconds. Add the dried fruits and almonds, and sauté over medium heat for 2 minutes or until the nuts begin to brown.

4. Add the liquid ingredients to the pan, and simmer for 5 minutes over low heat. Lightly press down on the fruit to soften and blend their flavors. The sauce should thicken slightly.

5. Place the chicken pieces or shredded chicken into the pot. Using tongs or a large spoon, coat the chicken well with the sauce. Reheat the chicken for 10–15 minutes until hot and flavorful. Adjust the seasonings if needed.

6. Serve over pasta, rice, or couscous.

YIELD: 4 SERVINGS

TINA'S TIDBITS

• *Young children should cut the dried fruits using a chef's knife guided with your hands so that their fingers are out of the way. Older children may have more control with a 5-inch utility knife.*

• *Younger children can work at the stove provided they are on a sturdy stool that makes the stovetop level with their waist and you are helping them stabilize the frying pan and/or putting your arm around their waist to ensure their safety.*

Kitchen Conversations

● Today there is much discussion about people going hungry or eating "junk" food that has calories but no nutrition. People are often too busy to make a meal from scratch. Discuss the difference between convenient foods and convenience foods.

● How can convenient foods like mayonnaise, canned tuna fish, frozen or dried fruits and vegetables, and even roasted chicken help you eat healthier?

● MAZON: A Jewish Response to Hunger is a national nonprofit organization working to end hunger in the United States and Israel. MAZON and its supporters believe that it is the obligation of the Jewish community to provide for people who are hungry. Discuss feeding people and feeding people food that is good for them. Is there a difference? How can we as families help others?

Kugels

Hardly a Jewish holiday goes by without some form of kugel being served. Even Passover has its own kugel, made with small matzah pieces called farfel. So why is kugel so popular, and when did it start to be part of Jewish heritage?

Actually, our ancestors didn't start out to make anything resembling our modern-day kugel. Originally a seasoned ball of flour dough was placed in the top of a Sabbath stew. The pot was tightly covered, and the dough was steamed in the stew while it cooked slowly all night long. After Saturday morning Shabbat services, both the stew and the bread dumpling were eaten. This cooking technique originated in southern Germany about eight hundred years ago.

Soon Jewish cooks saw that the non-Jewish German cooks in their area were making steamed puddings in clay pots, so they took their flour dumpling batter and put it in a *kugeltopf* (*kugel* meant "ball," and *topf* meant "jar") and placed it in the center of the covered stew to steam all night.

When the southern German Jews moved eastward to Poland and Lithuania, they took their love of this steamed dumpling to their new communities. German Jews pronounced it *koogle*, which meant "ball" to them. Polish and Lithuanian Jews pronounced it *kugel*, meaning "pudding," and Galitzianers (people living in Galicia, an area stretching from southeastern Poland to southwestern Russia) referred to the pudding as *keegle*. By now, kugel was cooked outside of the stew and was seasoned with savory ingredients like onion and herbs and sometimes expensive spices like salt and pepper (yes, salt and pepper were prized spices!). Sweetened versions were also served when the cook could afford ingredients like honey, sugar, apples, and cinnamon.

Around the fifteenth century, the influence of trade from the Middle East saw the transformation of the kugel from bread to noodles and egg farfel (little flakes of pasta). *Lokshen* meant "noodles," and *lokshen kugel* established its permanence in Jewish culinary culture.

In the sixteenth century, the Ottoman Empire stretched into parts of Eastern Europe and introduced the people to rice and cornmeal. Rice puddings were initially firm baked dishes, not the creamy variety that is popular today. Cornmeal was not only used in porridges but baked to create dishes like Italian polenta.

By the early nineteenth century, potatoes became a main crop in Eastern Europe, and even poor Jews could manage to find some potatoes, onions, eggs, and goose fat to put together, so potato kugel became popular. When many of these Eastern European Jews came to live in North America, they brought their love of *lokshen kugel* and potato kugel with them, and we now see them at almost all Jewish celebrations.

In order to be considered a kugel and not a casserole or a cake, a kugel must contain four ingredients:

- A starch: flour, bread, noodles, rice, potatoes, or matzah
- Eggs: to hold the mixture together when baked
- Fat: oil, chicken fat, butter, margarine, or coconut oil
- Liquid: a small amount of water, broth, milk, or juice

How you pronounce the word and what ingredients you use in your favorite versions say a lot about where you come from. Your own family's kugel history makes for a great kitchen conversation, whether you're reflecting on generations of kugel tradition or starting your own.

Bread Kugel with Dried Fruit and Sun-Dried Tomatoes

*T**he first bread kugels made eight hundred years ago probably didn't have more than a few raisins in them. They definitely didn't have sun-dried tomatoes, since tomatoes were first brought to Europe from the Americas in the sixteenth century! This recipe combines many of the flavors and foods found in Spain and Portugal (the home of Sephardic Jews) with the classic technique for making a bread kugel.*

3 tablespoons olive oil, plus additional
    for greasing the pan
1 onion, diced
2 ribs celery, chopped
1 cup chopped mushrooms
½ cup chopped mixed dried fruit
    (apples, prunes, pears, apricots, or
    any of your other favorites)
½ cup dried sweetened cranberries
1 cup apricot nectar
¼ cup Madeira (optional; add more
    apricot nectar if not using)
¼ cup sun-dried tomatoes packed in
    oil, drained and chopped
½ cup toasted almonds, coarsely
    chopped

1 loaf of white bread or challah with
    crust, cut into ½-inch cubes (about
    7 cups)
1 teaspoon dried thyme
½ teaspoon crushed rosemary
½ teaspoon sage
¼ teaspoon marjoram
¼ teaspoon nutmeg
Kosher salt and 10 grindings of pepper
    to taste
1½ cups chicken broth, warm or at
    room temperature
1 egg

1. Sauté the onion in the olive oil until lightly golden. Add the celery and mushrooms, and sauté for about 10 minutes or until the vegetables are soft and have given up their juices. Set aside.

2. Grease a 2-quart casserole or 11½ x 8-inch pan with some additional olive oil.

3. Combine the chopped dried fruit, dried cranberries, apricot nectar, and Madeira in a small glass bowl, and microwave on high for 2 minutes. Set aside.

4. Combine the sun-dried tomatoes, almonds, and bread cubes in a 4-quart bowl.

5. Mix the seasonings with the chicken broth and egg. Set aside.

6. Add the onion mixture and the dried fruit/juice mixture to the bowl with the bread cubes and toss.

7. Add the broth and egg mixture, and stir until the mixture is very moist and almost runny. If necessary, add a little more broth or nectar.

8. Pour the mixture into the prepared casserole, and bake at 350°F for 30–40 minutes.

NOTE: The casserole can be baked for the first 25 minutes covered with foil, shiny side up. Then remove the foil for the remainder of the cooking time. This will give you a very soft stuffing.

YIELD: 12 OR MORE SERVINGS

TINA'S TIDBITS

- *Don't be put off by the number of ingredients. Each step can be worked on independently over the course of the day, covered, and then all combined before baking.*
- *Cream sherry or additional apricot nectar can be substituted for the Madeira if you prefer.*
- *Eliminating the sun-dried tomatoes reduces saltiness, so adjust the seasonings accordingly if you don't include them.*
- *You may substitute 2 teaspoons of poultry seasoning mix for the individual herbs if you prefer.*

Kitchen Conversations

● Do you think the Jews of Eastern Europe would use apricots and other dried fruits or apples, pears, and raisins? Why?

● Using popular, modern ingredients such as Madeira and sun-dried tomatoes along with dried cranberries in this classic form of kugel shows how recipes change over time with access to new and/or different available ingredients. Are there any family recipes that your relatives have changed because they couldn't find a certain ingredient or because they liked one food more than another?

● How would you change this recipe to include ingredients you like that are available where you live?

Zella's Classic Noodle Kugel

*J*ewish celebrations always seem to revolve around food. Sharing, nurturing, and giving thanks have all been expressed on Jewish tables overflowing with food! Even in ancient times Jews would travel to the Temple for harvest festivals to give thanks to God for their good crops.

Many Jewish cooks went into catering, and the most famous caterer in Dallas, Texas, was Zella Sobel z"l. This recipe was famous, and some Dallasites can even proclaim that this kugel was served at their naming, bar mitzvah, and wedding and all prepared by the same wonderful woman.

12-ounce bag medium egg noodles
1 stick unsalted butter
8 ounces cream cheese
¾ cup sugar
16 ounces cottage cheese

8 ounces sour cream or Greek yogurt
1 teaspoon vanilla
4 large eggs
15-ounce can sliced peaches in juice,
   drained

Topping:

½ stick unsalted butter
1 cup cornflake crumbs
½ cup sugar
2 teaspoons cinnamon

1. Preheat the oven to 350°F. Butter a 13 x 9-inch (3-quart) glass casserole and set aside.

2. Cook the noodles according to package directions for 8 minutes or until soft. Drain in a colander but do not rinse. Place in a large mixing bowl.

3. While the noodles are cooking, place the butter, cream cheese, and sugar in a food processor work bowl, and pulse on and off until there are no big chunks of butter.

4. Add the cottage cheese, sour cream or yogurt, vanilla, and eggs, and process until the mixture is smooth. You might want to stop once and scrape down the sides of the work bowl with a rubber spatula.

5. Add the drained peaches to the work bowl; pulse on and off 10 times to chop the peaches. Add the mixture to the noodles, and stir with a rubber spatula to combine. Pour into the prepared pan and bake for 30 minutes.

6. To make the topping, melt the butter in a small glass dish in the microwave. Mix the topping ingredients in a 1-quart bowl, and mix in the melted butter. Set aside.

7. After the kugel has baked for 30 minutes, carefully remove it from the oven, spread the cornflake topping over the top, and return it to the oven for 10 more minutes or until the topping is golden.

YIELD: 12 OR MORE SERVINGS

Kitchen Conversations

- Almost every family has a favorite cheese kugel recipe. What is yours? What is different about your recipe?

- Sometimes people can't eat dairy products. Can you think of ways to make this recipe without them? What could you substitute for the cheeses and the butter?

TINA'S TIDBITS

- *Never allow children under the age of ten to drain hot liquid from a large pot, as their faces may be too close to the hot steam rising, and it could burn them. They can, however, place the food into the hot liquid if they are tall enough or on a stable stool.*
- *Always remove the blade from the food processor before pouring out the contents into a mixing bowl. This prevents surprise splatters from the falling blade and, of course, prevents cuts.*
- *If you do not have cornflake crumbs available, take any flake cereal, put it in a sealed ziplock plastic bag, and let the children roll a rolling pin over it to make crumbs.*
- *Children under the age of five can make the kugel and the topping but should not sprinkle the topping on the hot dish unless an adult is holding their hand and steadying them on a stool. This will prevent burns from accidentally touching the hot pan.*

Pareve Apple Raisin Kugel

Did you know that Adam and Eve's "apple" was most likely a fig or a grape? And when King Solomon's poem Song of Songs talked about the beautiful smell from the apple, it wasn't really an apple because apples weren't grown in the region at that time and they don't have a strong aroma?

Because no fruits listed in the Bible grew in Europe or Russia, where the large Ashkenazic communities lived, the apple became an important symbol of Jewish renewal and ritual. Apples were harvested just in time for Rosh HaShanah—a new fruit for a new year. Apples also stored well over the winter and could be used to make charoset for Passover. In the poorest Jewish communities, apples were the special ingredient that made a simple dish into a festive treat. Because of this, apples were often added to a plain lokshen kugel (noodle kugel) to make it special for Shabbat dinner. Eaten with a meat dinner, the kugel couldn't contain any cheese or butter. Here is a basic apple kugel worthy of your Shabbat table.

---

4 large eggs

¼ cup corn oil or other flavorless
   vegetable oil

½ cup unsweetened applesauce

¼ cup brown sugar

12 ounces wide noodles

2 unpeeled Fuji or Gala apples

¾ cup dark raisins

2 tablespoons sugar mixed with ½
   teaspoon cinnamon

---

1. Lightly grease an 11 x 7-inch (2-quart) glass casserole with nonstick spray. Preheat the oven to 350°F.

2. Using a wire whisk, whisk together the eggs, oil, applesauce, and brown sugar in a 4-quart mixing bowl until thick and creamy.

3. Cook the noodles in boiling salted water according to package directions. Drain in a colander, and add to the egg mixture.

4. Core and cut the apples into sections and the sections into 1-inch chunks. Add these and the raisins to the noodles. Mix well and pour into the greased pan.

5. Sprinkle with the sugar/cinnamon mixture, and bake in the oven for 40 minutes or until golden and firm.

YIELD: 6-8 SERVINGS

TINA'S TIDBITS

• *Small snack containers of applesauce often put in school lunches are the right amount for this recipe.*

• *An apple corer/slicer is the perfect tool to use with children. Older children are strong enough to press down on the apple on their own, but younger children will need some help. Put your hands on the utensil first and have the child push down on your hands, not the other way around. You could hurt a child's hand if yours were on top pushing hard.*

• *Extra nutrients and flavor cells are found in apple peel, and avoiding peeling apples is both a time saver and a safety issue. Most of the apple recipes in this book do not require peeling them for that reason.*

Kitchen Conversations

● If you were making this kugel in the fall, what other fruits could you use? What about the spring or summer?

● Could you add vegetables to the kugel? With or without some fruit? Share your ideas and see if you can create your own special kugel for Shabbat or a holiday.

Pareve Apricot Orange Noodle Kugel

*S*ince most kugels were originally meant to be served with a festive meat meal and in centuries past the only cooking fat available was goose or chicken fat, observant Jews did not use any dairy products in their recipes. Today we can use vegetable oil so that the dish is pareve (containing neither milk nor meat products).

    This is a modern recipe using fruit preserves and fruit juice to sweeten the dish. It is easy to make because no knife work is required. Perfect for very young cooks!

¾ cup orange juice

1 cup apricot preserves (about a
    12-ounce jar)

Two 4-ounce containers of
    unsweetened applesauce (or 1 cup)

1 teaspoon vanilla

1 teaspoon cinnamon

4 large eggs

¼ cup sugar

½ cup golden raisins (optional)

12 ounces extra wide egg noodles

Topping:

¼ cup sugar

½ teaspoon cinnamon

¼ teaspoon nutmeg

½ cup sliced almonds

2 tablespoons coconut oil or margarine

1. Preheat the oven to 350°F. Lightly oil a 12 x 8-inch (2-quart) casserole. Set aside.

2. Measure the orange juice in a 2-cup glass measuring cup. Add apricot preserves to the cup until the juice reaches the 1¾-cup line. Pour into a 4-quart mixing bowl, and add the next six ingredients. Whisk the mixture together well.

3. Cook the noodles according to package directions for 8 minutes or until soft. Drain in a colander but do not rinse. Using a rubber spatula, gently combine the noodles with the apricot mixture in the mixing bowl.

4. Pour the noodles into the greased casserole. Cover with foil, dull side facing up. Bake for 35 minutes.

5. While the kugel is baking, prepare the topping. Combine the topping ingredients in a 1-quart bowl. Use your fingertips to blend all the ingredients together. Set aside.

6. After 35 minutes, remove the kugel from the oven and discard the foil. Sprinkle the topping mixture evenly over the top, and return the pan to the oven for an additional 15–20 minutes or until the top and sides are golden. Remove from the oven, let the kugel rest for 10 minutes, then cut into pieces and serve.

YIELD: 8 SERVINGS

- *Because this recipe is good for younger children, it is best to remember that they can put the noodles into the water but must not be too close when the boiling water is drained from the noodles.*

- *Always have children stand on a sturdy stool or step stool. Never have them kneeling on a chair. If you only have a chair for them to stand on, it must have four legs so it won't rock or tip.*

- *It is best to buy the almonds sliced so no chopping is required. However, if you buy slivered or whole almonds that need to be chopped, with supervision even a very young child can chop the nuts using a chef's knife and the rocking motion to break the nuts into small pieces.*

Kitchen Conversations

- Discuss kashrut (keeping kosher). Name some foods that are or contain meat. Name some dairy foods and some foods around the house that are neutral, or pareve.

- This dish is pareve. What would make it a meat dish? A dairy dish?

Delicious and Easy Rice Kugel

Rice originated in India and China, and its cultivation spread to Persia more than two thousand years ago. The Arabs learned how to grow rice from the Persians, and when they conquered Spain, Sicily, the Middle East, and North Africa, they introduced rice cultivation to these regions. Jewish cooks living in these areas included rice in their dishes, and rice was regularly served for Shabbat. When the Jews were forced out of Spain, they brought their knowledge of rice cookery with them and introduced many recipes to other parts of Europe. Rice's popularity for Shabbat found its way into kugel recipes, replacing noodles as the primary starch.

This recipe is delicious, and it is easy. The only difficult task for a young cook is separating the eggs, but that is it! A wonderful, thin custard layer forms on the top of the baked kugel. This is a rice pudding that you cut, not spoon into a serving dish, and it can be served warm or cold.

½ **cup basmati rice**
1 **cup water**
½ **cup raisins**
¼ **cup water**
1½ **cups low-fat milk (1–2%)**
½ **cup half-and-half**
2 **egg yolks**
1 **whole egg**

½ **cup sugar**
⅛ **teaspoon kosher salt**
Zest of ½ medium orange
¼ **teaspoon nutmeg**
½ **teaspoon cinnamon**
1 **teaspoon vanilla**
Butter for greasing baking dish

1. Combine the rice and the 1 cup water in a 2-quart saucepan with a lid. Bring to a boil, cover, reduce heat to low, and cook for 16 minutes. Set aside.

2. Place the raisins and ¼ cup water in a small glass bowl, and microwave on high for 45 seconds. Set aside for the raisins to absorb water. Drain before using if all of the water hasn't been absorbed.

3. Preheat the oven to 325°F. Grease a 2-quart porcelain soufflé dish with butter. Set aside.

4. Place all the remaining ingredients into a 3-quart bowl, and whisk with a wire whisk to thoroughly combine. Add the rice and drained raisins. Pour into the greased soufflé dish, and bake for 45 minutes or until golden.

YIELD: 8 SERVINGS

TINA'S TIDBITS

- *To make this recipe even easier, you can use leftover rice from Chinese take-out! Although not the nutty Basmati rice, this rice is medium grain and sticky and perfect to use. Just measure 1½ cups of rice and you are good to go!*
- *Never use instant or converted rice for kugels, because they do not contain enough starch to make the cooked mixture firm.*
- *Remember, do not let a young child remove anything hot from the microwave oven, and make sure that the microwave is below chest height for an older child to safely use it.*
- *The half-and-half really is necessary because it creates a custard layer on the top of the finished kugel. If you must, you may use 2 cups of milk instead of the combination of milk and cream.*
- *Using a heavy soufflé dish eliminates the need for a hot-water bath around the baking kugel, which is a common method for cooking custards. This is very important when cooking with children, as scalding hot water requires complete attention when removing the dish from the oven and could be hazardous around children.*

Kitchen Conversations

- Recipes often change when the cook moves to a different part of the country or region of the world. What ingredients could you add or change in this recipe to make it better reflect your hometown or the country where your ancestors came from?

- Why do you think some rice puddings are baked and others are made on the top of the stove? How does the country of origin or the prosperity of the community affect how a simple rice dish is cooked?

Potato Onion Kugel

Potato kugel did not become popular until the nineteenth century, when potatoes were grown throughout Europe and Western Russia. By the end of that century the poor were eating potatoes two or more times a day! However, on Shabbat even poor Jews found an extra egg, onion, and possibly some pepper to raise the lowly potato to new heights. When Jewish immigrants came to North America, they brought the potato recipes they knew and loved with them. Even the popular potato knish of today is a variation of the Shabbat potato kugel brought here over one hundred years ago.

2 tablespoons extra virgin olive oil

2 tablespoons rendered chicken fat or extra virgin olive oil

3 medium onions, diced into ½-inch pieces (6 cups total)

3 pounds unpeeled California long white or Yukon Gold potatoes (about 12 small)

2½ cups matzah farfel

8 large eggs

1½ tablespoons kosher salt

25 grindings of black pepper or to taste

Additional chicken fat or olive oil for greasing pan and top

1. Preheat oven to 350°F.

2. Heat a 10- or 12-inch skillet on high for 15 seconds. Add olive oil and chicken fat, and heat until the fat is melted.

3. Add the onions and stir to coat with the fat mixture. Cover the pan and cook on medium high for 5 minutes.

4. Remove the cover and sauté the onions for 3 more minutes until just beginning to turn golden.

5. Grate the potatoes using the fine grating disk on your food processor or a medium grater if shredding by hand, and immediately put in a colander.

6. Run water through the potatoes to remove starch and whiten them. Press down on the potatoes and drain thoroughly. Set aside.

7. Place the matzah farfel in a 4-quart bowl. Cover with warm water and let rest for 3 minutes or until the farfel is soft. If any water remains, drain thoroughly. Add the eggs, salt, and pepper to the farfel, and beat with a fork until well combined. Add the sautéed onion and mix again.

8. Add the grated potato. Use your hand and a fork to work the potatoes into the mixture until all the ingredients are evenly mixed. The mixture might look dry at first, but soon it will appear moist and pourable.

9. Grease a 13 x 9-inch (3-quart) glass casserole with a little chicken fat (or olive oil). Pour in the potato mixture, and lightly spread it evenly with the fork. Do not pack down the potato mixture.

10. Put an additional tablespoon of chicken fat or oil in your hand and rub the oil evenly over the top of the potatoes in the pan.

11. Cover the pan with aluminum foil, dull side up. Bake for 25 minutes. Remove the foil and continue to bake another 25–30 minutes or until the top is golden and the kugel is firm to the touch. If the kugel is done but hasn't browned, you may place it under the broiler until golden.

YIELD: 12 SERVINGS

Kitchen Conversations

● What do you think your ancestors did with leftover potato kugel? How could you eat the leftovers? Should you reheat them, fry them with some onions, eat them with ketchup like French fries? How about wrapping them in pastry and baking them? Sound weird? Well, maybe that is how the potato knish was invented!

TINA'S TIDBITS

• *California white or Yukon Gold potatoes are good to use when cooking with children. The hard flesh does not discolor as rapidly as a russet potato, and the skin is so thin that neither variety of potato requires peeling! No peeling means it's safer and more nutritious.*
• *If you do not have a food processor, try to find a plastic, medium-holed grater if you are grating by hand. Children are less likely to cut their knuckles using a hard plastic grater than a metal one.*
• *Covering the pan with foil dull side up helps the pan absorb heat faster while preventing the contents from drying out.*

Part III

JUST FOR PASSOVER

PASSOVER MIGAS
PAGE 122

There is no better time to engage a child in the culinary traditions of the Jewish world than at Passover. Passover involves children in many ways. The theatrics of searching for *chameitz* (leavened food) with a candle and a feather before the beginning of the holiday, decorating the table with Passover symbols like little toy frogs or insect stickers on place cards, or helping to make the *charoset* are fun activities and can have a strong impact on children's holiday memories. Reciting the Four Questions and searching for the *afikoman* continue their immersion in their Jewish heritage.

The completion of the seder meal does not mean the conclusion of activities for children. Children often visit relatives over the holiday, and meals and snacks need to be prepared for them. This is a perfect time, after all the hustle and bustle of preparing for the seder is done, to create in your kitchen. Chances are that leftovers will provide the mainstay for your meals, but what about breakfast, snacks, and treats?

This section will take you from alternative *charoset* recipes, to noshes for the seder table, to breakfast dishes and snacks. There is even an old Italian recipe to be served on the Shabbat before Passover that depicts the waters of the Sea of Reeds engulfing Pharaoh's armies. With a little creativity and some Passover noodles, this recipe can even be served during the holiday week.

Syrian Charoset

Charoset *is a blend of fruits, nuts, and spices served at Passover, to symbolize the cement that held the bricks together on Egyptian pyramids. It doesn't really look like cement, and it tastes much better! Every Jewish community has made its own special mixture to eat during the seder. Jews have lived in Syria since biblical times—that's more than four thousand years! Some of the best cooks came from the city of Aleppo. Today there are fewer than thirty Jews in the whole country, but this recipe keeps their history alive.*

8 ounces Medjool dates, pitted

6 ounces dried apricots

1 cup golden raisins

1½ cups water

½ cup almonds, toasted

½ cup shelled pistachio nuts, unsalted

3 tablespoons honey

¼ cup brown sugar or to taste

Zest of ½ orange

1½ teaspoons cinnamon

1½ teaspoons orange blossom water

2 tablespoons sweet Passover wine or as needed

Cinnamon for dusting

1. Place the dates, apricots, and raisins in a 2-quart saucepan. Add the water and simmer until the fruit is soft and the liquid is almost all absorbed, leaving a little syrup behind.

2. Place the contents of the pan into a processor work bowl and pulse the machine on and off until coarsely chopped.

3. Add the nuts, honey, brown sugar, zest, and cinnamon, and process the mixture until it becomes a paste.

4. Add the orange blossom water and 2 tablespoons of the wine to the paste, and pulse the machine on and off until combined. If necessary, add more wine to achieve the desired consistency. Store in the refrigerator overnight or longer to let the fruit and spice flavors blend.

5. To serve, place in a bowl and sprinkle some additional cinnamon on top.

YIELD: 12+SERVINGS

- *This is a very easy recipe to make with children, because it requires no knife skills.*
- *Although not necessary, young children can pull the apricots and dates apart to process more easily and also to find any pits in the large dates.*
- *When using a food processor around children, always keep the plunger in the feed tube. Their fingers and hands are small and can fit inside the tube if they are curious.*

Kitchen Conversations

● Why is some *charoset* made with apples, pears, and bananas and others are made with dried apricots, dates, and figs?

● If you were to make up your own recipe for *charoset*, what fruits, nuts, and seasonings would you use?

Passover Migas

Migas are scrambled eggs with meats or vegetables topped with cheese. In Spain and Portugal, they were originally made with leftover bread, but in Mexico and the southwestern United States, it became popular to use leftover tortilla strips in the egg mixture. To replace the tortilla strips during Passover, I add matzah farfel for the crunch. They're easy to make, but don't forget to make enough to share!

1 teaspoon butter

1 teaspoon olive oil

½ yellow or red bell pepper, cut into strips

8 cherry or grape tomatoes, washed and left whole

1 large egg

¼ cup milk

¼ teaspoon ground cumin

3 shakes of garlic powder

Salt and freshly ground pepper to taste

⅓ cup matzah farfel

¼ cup shredded mozzarella or cheddar cheese (optional)

Tomato salsa (optional)

1. Heat an 8-inch nonstick pan for 20 seconds. Add butter and olive oil, and heat for 10 seconds. Add the peppers and tomatoes to the pan, and using a wooden spoon or large metal stirring spoon, sauté for 3–4 minutes over medium-high heat. The peppers should be soft and dark in spots, and the tomatoes should be soft when pressed with the spoon.

2. Using a fork, mix the egg, milk, cumin, garlic powder, and salt and pepper in a 1-quart bowl. Add the matzah farfel and stir to coat the farfel completely with the egg mixture.

3. Add the egg mixture to the frying pan with the vegetables, and gently stir with a big spoon until no liquid remains and the eggs are firm and completely cooked. If using the cheese, add it to the pan, stir once or twice, and then remove from heat.

4. Serve as is or with some tomato salsa.

YIELD: 1 SERVING

NOTE: This recipe may be doubled or tripled. Just adjust the size of the pan you are using.

TINA'S TIDBITS

- *Any vegetables can be used— leftover broccoli, cooked carrots, olives, scallions—but no more than ¾ cup total. This is a good way to introduce new vegetables to a child.*
- *Cutting fresh bell peppers is much easier if the pepper is cut in half from stem to bottom, laid skin side down on the cutting board, and cut from the inside out.*
- *Although this mixture shouldn't spatter, young children (five and under) should be standing on a step stool a few feet away from the stove when you sauté the vegetables. Once the egg mixture is added, the step stool can be brought to the stove for the young cook to stir.*
- *Never allow a child to sit on the counter near the stove in order to see!*

Kitchen Conversations

● The first Jews to live in Mexico were Conversos, Jews who attempted to practice their religion in secret when they were barred from doing so during the Spanish Inquisition. Throughout history, many Jewish people have had to keep their Jewish identity a secret at times when they could be punished for being Jewish. What would you have to do differently to hide being Jewish?

● How would you celebrate Passover in secret?

● How would you observe Shabbat in secret?

● What would be the hardest part?

● What would be the easiest part?

Matzah Brie

*T*his recipe is quite easy to make with children. It is just hard to describe! Everyone has their own family favorite. Even after looking at cookbooks from over one hundred years ago and many written in the 1930s, when European Jewish immigrants' recipes were published, I find it hard to define *matzah brie.* Brie *is German and means "wide." My theory is that since the broken pieces of matzah bound together with egg create a wide or broad pancake, the dish got its name from that definition.*

Some matzah brie *is made without water, with dry sheets of matzah dipped in egg and then fried. Most recipes call for soaking, washing, or sprinkling the sheets of matzah with water before proceeding. Egg batter seasoned with salt and pepper and no sugar probably had its origins in Germany, Lithuania, or Russia. Those who sweetened their batter with sugar and spice probably have roots in Poland, Hungary, and other areas known in the past as Galicia. Almost everyone uses jam, cinnamon and sugar, or syrup as a topping.*

Here's my basic recipe. (Can you tell that half of my ancestors came from Poland?)

---

2 sheets of plain matzah (egg matzah may be used, but it falls apart pretty fast)

1 egg

¼ cup milk

¼ teaspoon salt

1–2 teaspoons sugar, according to taste

¼ teaspoon vanilla

1 tablespoon unsalted butter

---

1. Fill a 2-quart bowl with very warm tap water. Break each matzah into roughly 4 pieces and place in the bowl. Press down so that the water covers the matzah.

2. Mix the egg, milk, salt, sugar, and vanilla in a 1-quart mixing bowl.

3. Drain the matzah in a colander, and gently press down on the matzah to remove the water. Add the matzah to the egg mixture, and stir carefully with a fork so that egg coats all of the matzah.

4. Heat an 8-inch nonstick frying pan for 10 seconds. Add the butter and swirl about in the pan until melted. Add the egg/matzah, and gently press to form one large pancake.

5. Cook until the bottom is golden, and then turn it over with a wide metal spatula or turner. (See Tina's Tidbits for the best technique for this.) When the bottom is crisp, remove from the pan, cut into wedges, and serve with topping of your choice.

YIELD: 2-4 SERVINGS

Kitchen Conversations

● What are your family *matzah brie* traditions? Does everyone agree on the recipe? Which version is your favorite?

● Experiment with different ingredients. Could you make this with vegetables? What about other spices, or a sweet and savory combination by adding pepper with the sugar? Create your own unique recipe. Type it up and save it to start a new family tradition.

TINA'S TIDBITS

It is easiest to flip the half-cooked brie by using two spatulas or flipping the pancake over onto a plate and then sliding it back into the pan uncooked side down. This second method should NOT be attempted by anyone under the age of 10 and is best demonstrated by an adult.

Ruota Del Faraone (Pharaoh's Wheels)

Getting your kitchen ready for Passover can be lots of work, but it can also be fun. Since noodles and other pasta products can't be eaten during Passover, Italian Jews prepare this pasta dish on the Shabbat before Pesach. But this is no ordinary pasta dish—it tells a story! Sauced thin pasta noodles are twirled into mounds to look like the waves in the parted Red Sea, and raisins and pine nuts are sprinkled around the pasta "waves" to represent the Egyptian soldiers drowning in the waters after the Jews escaped.

Pot roast gravy makes this dish very easy to make, but I have also included a classic recipe for a meat sauce to be used when pot roast is not served.

½ cup raisins

2 tablespoons extra virgin olive oil

2 tablespoons rendered chicken fat (or more oil)

2 large leaves of fresh sage or 1 teaspoon dried sage

4-inch sprig of fresh rosemary or 1 teaspoon dried rosemary

6 ounces turkey sausage, cut into ½-inch rounds, or ground turkey or beef

¼ cup white wine or 1 cup pot roast gravy

Salt and freshly ground pepper to taste

1 quart chicken broth

1 quart water

1 tablespoon extra virgin olive oil

1 tablespoon salt

8 ounces tagliatelle noodles (¼-inch wide flat noodles)

½ cup pine nuts, toasted

3 tablespoons dry bread crumbs or panko bread crumbs

1 teaspoon olive oil

1. If the raisins are hard, soak them in warm water while you prepare the pasta.

2. Turn the burner on the stove to high, and heat a 10-inch frying pan for 15 seconds.

3. Add the olive oil and chicken fat to the hot pan, and heat for another 10 seconds. Reduce the heat to medium.

4. Add the herbs, and stir once or twice to coat the herbs with oil. Add the sausage or meat, and using a large metal mixing spoon, sauté in the pan until the meat is no longer pink.

5. Add the wine or gravy, and mix and cook for 1–2 minutes until most of the liquid is absorbed. Set aside.

6. Meanwhile in a 4-quart pot, bring the chicken broth, water, 1 tablespoon olive oil, and 1 teaspoon salt to a boil. Add the noodles and cook according to package directions. When done, reserve ½ cup of the cooking liquid, and then drain the noodles in a colander.

7. Add the noodles and the reserved cooking liquid to the meat sauce, and gently stir to mix well. Add the drained raisins and pine nuts, and gently stir to combine. Add salt and pepper to taste.

8. Preheat the oven to 350°F. Lightly grease a 2-quart oval casserole with a little olive oil.

9. Scoop up some of the noodles into a ladle. Using a large turning fork, twist the noodles into a small mound and place the mound into the greased casserole. Repeat with the remaining noodles until you have lots of mounds that look like waves in the sea.

10. Combine the bread crumbs with the teaspoon of olive oil and sprinkle over the top.

11. Place the casserole in the hot oven and bake until the bread crumbs are lightly golden.

YIELD: 4 SERVINGS

Kitchen Conversations

● What do you do in your home to get ready for Passover?

● Does anyone in the family make a special dish before Passover to get rid of *chameitz*?

● Discuss what foods are not eaten for Passover. Can you pick out some of these foods from your pantry?

TINA'S TIDBITS

• *When working at the stove with young children, always have them standing on a sturdy stool with their waist at counter height.*
• *Never leave a child near the stove unattended. Have all your ingredients next to you in little glass bowls—pretend you're Julia Child!*
• *If you have forgotten something, turn off the stove and have the child come down from the stool.*
• *Children are easily distracted, so carry on any discussions about Passover before you start or after the dish is in the oven.*

Persian Cauliflower and Raisin Kuku

Kuku *might sound like a silly name, but it is a delicious omelet-like pancake made in Iran. Before 1935, Iran was called Persia, and Jewish people have lived in Persia for almost twenty-five hundred years! When King Solomon's Temple was destroyed in 586 BCE, thousands of Jews were exiled to Babylonia, which at that time included the lands of Persia. The story of Purim takes place in Persia, in the city of Shushan.*

Kuku are light and fluffy and often contain vegetables and green herbs. Here are two recipes, one using cauliflower and one with spinach. Persians introduced the Moors to spinach, and cauliflower was introduced to Persian cuisine from neighboring Asia Minor (present-day Turkey). After the Moors conquered Spain, they introduced the vegetables to the Jews, and along with raisins, they were favored by the Spanish Moors and Jews for centuries. Although the Jews were exiled from Spain in 1492, their cooking traditions continued. So whenever you see a recipe that combines raisins with spinach or cauliflower, you can tell that it is a dish with Jewish connections!

Najmieh Batmanglij is my (and most Americans') go-to authority on Persian cuisine. Her recipes inspired me to create the following.

Kuku can be served hot out of the oven, at room temperature, or cold. This is a perfect recipe to make with children because it can be served whenever you have time to eat it as a snack or rewarmed as a light lunch or brunch dish.

20-ounce bag frozen cauliflower (or ½ head of large cauliflower)

2 medium onions

5 tablespoons extra virgin olive oil, divided use

1½ teaspoons kosher salt

2 small cloves of garlic, finely chopped or put through a garlic press

5 large eggs

Freshly ground black pepper, about 15 turns of a pepper mill

½ teaspoon turmeric

½ teaspoon cumin

3 tablespoons dark raisins

---

1. If the cauliflower is fresh, then chop into small pieces; if frozen, defrost and drain in a colander. Cut the onions in half top to bottom and then thinly slice. You should have about 4 cups.

2. Heat a large frying pan on high for 15 seconds. Add 3 tablespoons of oil and heat for 10 seconds more. Lower the heat to medium. Add the cauliflower, onions, and salt to the pan, stir to combine, cover the pan, and then cook for 3 minutes.

3. Uncover the pan and sauté until the cauliflower is soft and the onions are light golden brown. Add the garlic, and cook 1 minute more. Do not burn the garlic.

3. Transfer the cauliflower/onion mixture to a large mixing bowl, and mash with a potato masher until the cauliflower becomes a coarse puree. Set aside.

4. Preheat the oven to 350°F. Grease a 1½-quart casserole or 10-inch glass pie plate with the additional 2 tablespoons of oil.

5. Using a fork, combine the eggs, pepper, turmeric, cumin, and raisins in a 1-quart bowl with the cauliflower and mix to thoroughly combine.

6. Pour the egg mixture into the greased casserole or pie plate, and bake on the center shelf of the oven for 30 minutes or until the top is golden and the eggs are cooked in the center. Serve immediately or at room temperature.

NOTE: Cut the cooled kuku into 1-inch squares, and place on a plate with toothpicks for bite-sized snacks or appetizers during the seder or anytime you need hors d'oeuvres.

YIELD: 4–6 SERVINGS

Kitchen Conversations

Create your own *kuku*. What vegetable or vegetables would you like to use? What spices would make it taste good?

TINA'S TIDBITS

- *This is a good recipe to introduce cooking at the stove because the mixture won't splatter and scare a young child.*
- *It is very important that the child be standing on a stable surface—**chairs are not appropriate!***
- *Make sure that the stove is at least at midriff height. Faces should be far away from cooking utensils.*
- *Hot casseroles should be removed from the oven by an adult or a supervised child over the age of ten.*

Persian Kuku with Spinach, Pine Nuts, and Raisins

*T*his recipe for kuku *combines some of the foods that the Moors brought from Persia and the Middle East and introduced to Jewish people living in Spain. When, in 1492, the Jews were no longer allowed to live in Spain, they brought their love of spinach, raisins, and pine nuts with them to Italy.*

2 tablespoons extra virgin olive oil

10 ounces frozen chopped spinach, defrosted

¼ cup toasted pine nuts

¼ cup raisins

½ cup finely chopped chives or the green part of scallions

1½ teaspoons kosher salt

10 grindings of black pepper or to taste

1 teaspoon ground cumin

¼ teaspoon garlic powder

½ teaspoon Persian advieh, baharat, or cinnamon

1 pinch of nutmeg

5 eggs

2 tablespoons matzah meal

1. Add all of the oil to the pan and coat well. The excess oil will help cook the kuku.

2. Place the defrosted chopped spinach in a colander. Take small handfuls of the spinach and squeeze very hard until almost all of the moisture has drained. Place the spinach in a medium bowl.

3. Add the rest of the ingredients to the spinach, and mix with a fork until the mixture is well combined.

4. Pour into the prepared pan and place on the middle shelf of the oven. Bake for 30 minutes or until the top of the kuku begins to brown.

5. Remove from the oven, cool, and cut into 1-inch squares.

YIELD: 8 OR MORE FOR APPETIZERS, 6–8 AS A SIDE DISH

- *Advieh and* baharat *are the names for Persian and Middle Eastern spice mixtures that are used to flavor dishes. The name* baharat *comes from the Arabic word* bahar, *meaning "allspice." Columbus brought allspice back from the New World, thinking it was pepper. When the Arabs discovered it was a spice whose flavor tasted like a mixture of cloves and cinnamon, they named the spice* bahar *or "allspice." Today each region and each home in the Middle East has its own signature spice mixture.*

- *To see if this or any other egg custard is done, place a thin, sharp knife into the center of the dish. If the knife comes out clean, the custard is done. A toothpick is not useful for checking.*

- *Remove a dish from the oven to test it to see if it is done. Adult supervision must always be used when going to the oven. Never leave the oven door open while you are testing a baked product. This lets heat escape and triggers the oven to recycle and be hot, and it is very dangerous with young children and pets walking around the kitchen.*

Kitchen Conversations

● Look at a map and draw a line with a pencil or your finger from Persia to Spain to Italy to wherever you live. How far do you think this recipe traveled to get to you?

● Does your family have a favorite egg dish? Can you draw a line on a map from where the ingredients were first popular to where your family introduced it to your country and city?

Double Coconut Chocolate Macaroons

Macaroons, cookies generally made from ground almonds, sugar, and egg whites, are popular for Passover because the recipe doesn't use flour. But did you know that coconut macaroons only became popular about one hundred years ago? Coconuts had to be peeled and grated at home; you couldn't buy grated coconut in packages like today. However, that all changed in 1897 when Franklin Baker of Philadelphia discovered how to grate coconuts by machine instead of by hand.

8 ounces almonds
1 cup sugar
2 cups lightly packed coconut
10 ounces semisweet chocolate chips
    or 9 ounces dark chocolate
    (60% cocoa butter)

3 egg whites (approximately ⅓ cup)
⅓ cup coconut milk (unsweetened)
1 teaspoon almond extract

1. Place the almonds in a processor work bowl, and pulse the machine on and off until the nuts are finely chopped. Add the sugar and coconut, and pulse once or twice to combine.

2. If not using chips, break the chocolate into pieces before melting. Melt the chocolate in the microwave for 1 minute at 80 percent power and then 45 seconds at 50 percent. (This time is approximate and will vary based on your microwave oven. It might take less time. Watch carefully and stir the chocolate after the first 45 seconds to check on the melting time.)

3. In a 1-cup glass measuring cup, combine the egg whites, coconut milk, and almond extract. Set aside.

4. Add the melted chocolate to the nut mixture in the processor work bowl.

5. With the motor running, pour the egg white mixture into the work bowl and process until the dough comes together and is well combined. Place the dough in the freezer for 5 minutes or until it is firm enough to handle.

6. Preheat the oven to 350°F.

7. Wet your hands or lightly coat them with oil. (The dough is very sticky.)

8. Scoop up 1 tablespoon of the dough, and shape into a ball the size of a small walnut. Place on a cookie sheet lined with parchment paper. Repeat with the remaining dough.

9. Bake the macaroons for 12–15 minutes. (Convection ovens only need about 10–12 minutes at 350°F.) Do not overbake, as the cookie will harden more when the chocolate solidifies at room temperature.

10. Cool completely and then store at room temperature in an airtight container or freeze until needed.

YIELD: 5 DOZEN MACAROONS

Kitchen Conversations

- Coconut milk isn't milk at all (see note under Tina's Tidbits, below) and is in fact pareve, meaning it is vegetable-based and nondairy, and so can be eaten with either meat or dairy according to the laws of kashrut.

- What are some of your favorite pareve foods?

TINA'S TIDBITS

Most coconut milk is just coconut and water and comes from Thailand. There is no Hecksher on it, but I treat it as an unprocessed canned fruit for Passover. If that does not conform to your observance, combine 1 cup of coconut and ½ cup water in a blender (NOT processor) and blend until coconut is fairly pulverized. Strain mixture, pressing hard on the coconut solids to extract as much flavor as possible. Discard the solids and use liquid in the recipe.

Passover Granola

Sometimes, when Passover occurs during a school week, there just isn't enough time to make *matzah brie* or *matzah meal pancakes for breakfast. However, here is a great recipe to have on hand all week long!*

This granola is delicious with milk for breakfast and, eaten as is, makes for a healthy snack for school or work. If you want to satisfy your sweet tooth further, make the chocolate granola treats at the end of this recipe.

3 cups matzah farfel

⅔ cup sliced almonds

½ cup sweetened or unsweetened coconut

⅔ cup pecans, broken into large pieces

¼ teaspoon salt

1½ teaspoons cinnamon

¼ teaspoon nutmeg

6 tablespoons unsalted butter, pareve margarine, or coconut oil

⅓ cup wildflower or clover honey

1½ cups chopped dried mixed fruit of your choice (including raisins) or 7-ounce bag of dried fruit pieces

1. Preheat the oven to 325°F.

2. Mix the farfel, almonds, coconut, pecans, salt, cinnamon, and nutmeg in a 3-quart mixing bowl.

3. Melt the butter and honey in a small glass bowl in a microwave for 1 minute, until the butter is melted and the honey is more fluid.

4. Using a rubber spatula, stir the butter mixture into the farfel mixture until all the farfel is lightly coated with the butter.

5. Spread the mixture in a large jellyroll pan with 1-inch sides, and bake for 15 minutes. Halfway through baking quickly remove the pan from the oven, stir so the mixture browns evenly, and then return the pan to the oven for another 8 minutes, until the farfel is golden brown.

6. Remove the pan from the oven. Cool to room temperature, and then toss with the dried fruit.

7. When totally cooled, store in a ziplock bag or airtight storage container for all eight days of Passover (if it lasts that long).

Chocolate Granola Treats

1. Melt 8 ounces of Passover chocolate chips in the microwave or over a pot of hot, but not boiling, water. Using a rubber spatula, mix the melted chocolate with 2 cups prepared granola. Stir to coat well.

2. Drop by the teaspoonful onto parchment paper, and allow the mounds to firm up before you devour them!

Kitchen Conversations

● When my children were little, I adapted their favorite breakfast food so they could eat it for Passover. What do you normally eat for breakfast? Is there a way you can change it to be kosher for Passover? Can you think of a recipe for Passover French toast? For Passover pancakes? For Passover omelettes? Do you have to change many of the ingredients?

TINA'S TIDBITS

• *Passover granola is great to make with children of all ages. It's an excellent recipe for teaching measuring and mixing. Allow only older children to stir the granola halfway through baking and only if you remove the pan from the oven and close the oven door. The pan is hot, but children might forget that and touch the pan when stirring.*

• *Only older children should be allowed to remove hot butter/honey from the microwave, using pot holders, as the mixture is quite hot.*

• *If your microwave oven is higher than eye level for any age child,* **never** *let them remove anything after cooking. This is very dangerous!*

• *The same is true for any oven whose shelf is not at waist height or below. Their arms aren't long enough to reach the shelf if it is too high.*

• *To prevent burning the nuts, never pre-roast them if they will be baked in the oven.*

Geshmirta Matzah

Geshmirta matzah *is a funny-sounding name, but it is so delicious!* Geshmirta *is a Yiddish word that means something spread on top of something else. Yiddish was the language of Ashkenazic Jews living in Eastern Europe and Western Russia. Many of these Jews immigrated to South Africa, and this dish is very popular in Cape Town. I first heard about it from a friend of mine, but recently a reader wrote me to help her re-create a special food memory for her. I did. She loved it. Here's the recipe!*

3-4 sheets of matzah

8 ounces whipped cream cheese

1 egg

½ teaspoon vanilla extract

2 tablespoons sugar

2 tablespoons sour cream, cream, or
   Greek yogurt

2 tablespoons sugar mixed with ½
   teaspoon cinnamon

1. Preheat oven to 350°F. Line a jellyroll pan with foil, dull side up. Cover the foil with matzah, breaking pieces if necessary, to fit the entire bottom of the pan. Set aside.

2. Using a rubber spatula, mix the cream cheese, egg, vanilla, first 2 tablespoons of sugar, and sour cream or cream or yogurt in a 2-quart bowl until smooth and well combined.

3. Spread the mixture evenly over the matzah (if you have one, a small angled spatula would be perfect for younger children), and sprinkle with the remaining cinnamon sugar.

4. Bake for 15–20 minutes until the mixture is slightly golden and the matzah is crisp. Cut into squares and eat within an hour to preserve crispiness.

YIELD: 6-8 SERVINGS

Kitchen Conversations

● Do any adults in your family speak Yiddish?

● Do you know any Yiddish words? I bet you do. Have you ever heard the words *bagel*, *nosh*, *kvell*, *schlep*, or *tush*? They're all Yiddish words! *Bagel* means "ring," *nosh* means "to snack," *kvell* means "to be very proud, "*schlep* means "to carry or drag along," and *tush* comes from the word meaning "under."

TINA'S TIDBITS

• *Regular cream cheese may be used if at room temperature, but children will find it easier to blend the ingredients by hand using whipped cream cheese.*

• *Using softened ingredients at room temperature often eliminates the need for an electric mixer, making the recipe toddler friendly.*

Part IV

FUN
FOODS

POLPETTE POTENTINA,
PAGE 152

Jewish food need not be centered only around specific holidays. All of the places in the world where Jews have lived over the last thousand years have shaped the recipes and kitchen conversations in Jewish homes around the world. Cooking with children and teaching them the process that goes into making familiar foods like pizza, bagels, pretzels, hamburgers, and meatballs gives us a chance to see the world of the kitchen through their eyes and opens doors to their thoughts while they create, which lends itself to many wonderful conversations about the places we live now.

INDIAN LAMB MEATBALLS,
PAGE 150

Around the World, One Meatball at a Time

The use of ground meat is part of Jewish cooking everywhere around the world. The meat is almost always mixed with vegetables such as onions, carrots, or even eggplant and with starches like rice, bread, or other grains. The added ingredients help identify where the recipe originated. Bulgur? The Middle East. Rice? Eaten all along the silk trade route from Asia through Persia and the Levant and brought to Spain with the Moors. The spices added to the mix tell a story too. Cinnamon and allspice are favorite additions for Jews from Spain and Turkey. Allspice was brought to Europe by Columbus, and the Jews were significantly responsible for its trade and use in Spain and throughout the world after the expulsion of the Jews from Spanish territories in the 1500s. Cumin, ginger, and coriander are all used by Jews in North Africa as well as the Middle East. Fresh green herbs, or *sabzi*, are popular in Persian cuisine.

Ground meat can trace its origins to the 1200s, when Genghis Khan and his Mongol warriors conquered most of the known world from China to Europe. The warriors traveled on horseback and, not having time to stop and cook their food, would take bits of raw meat, press it into a disk, and then place it under their saddles on the horse's back. After hours or days of riding, the pounding of the saddle would make the meat tender, and the warrior would eat the meat without stopping to cook it! When the Mongols invaded Moscow, their food choices became popular, and the Russians called the raw, scraped meat steak Tartar (the Mongols were called Tartars in Russia).

Minced or hashed meat became popular in Europe, and by the 1400s, sausages were beginning to be made in a few countries. By the 1600s, the major European seaport of Hamburg, Germany, was sending sailors to Russia, where they discovered the raw meat patties. In Germany, the dish became known as Tartar steak.

Around the time of the American Revolution in the late 1700s, German sailors introduced the colonists to eating slightly cooked ground beef, but it wasn't until the early to mid-1800s that the Hamburg sailors coming to the port of New York really popularized this dish, which came to be known as Hamburg steak. Food trucks would set up near the docks, and to attract the German sailors, they would advertise "Steak cooked in the Hamburg style," which meant the meat was only slightly cooked on the outside and raw on the inside.

The German ships that brought immigrants to North America in the mid-1800s served a hard, salty, smoked beef that could withstand a long sea voyage. This was known as Hamburg beef and was prepared by shaving and mincing the meat and sometimes adding soaked bread crumbs and onion to it to stretch the amount of meat used in the recipe. Later the German emigrants transformed this dish by adding seasonings and bread crumbs to raw fresh meat and cooking it rare, and it became very popular.

In England, chopped meat, seasoned, shaped in an oval, and cooked well-done was called Salisbury steak because Dr. James Salisbury recommended eating this cooked meat three times a day to promote good health. But it wasn't until the 1904 Louisiana Purchase Exposition in St. Louis, Missouri (which also happens to be the birthplace of the ice-cream cone), that the first "hamburger" sandwich served between two slices of bread was officially born.

Meatballs, or as they were called in Persia, *kufteh* (which meant "pounded"), have long been very popular in the Arab world. When the Moors conquered Spain, they brought their food preferences with them. The Moors called the little meatballs *al-bunduqa,* which meant "hazelnut." The Spaniards named them *albondigas* and often made them walnut-sized to ease preparation. Spanish Jews often added bits of vegetables to the meat mixture and introduced nuts and spices to the mix. They didn't, however, use pork in the preparation, and this often was the evidence used against them during the Inquisition to prove that they weren't true converts to Christianity but were secretly practicing Jews.

Here are a few recipes, old and new, that have been influenced by Jewish cooks near and far. Enjoy!

Kyeftes de Karne kon Muezes (Meatballs with Nuts)

T*he Ladino name for this dish (also known as* albondigas de carne con nueces *in Spanish) is closely tied to the Turkish and Persian name for these spheres of ground meat. Ladino is the language spoken by Sephardic Jews, a mixture of Spanish and Hebrew along with a few elements derived from Turkish, Arabic, French, and other languages spoken in areas where Jews settled after the expulsion from Spain in 1492.*

This is my adaptation of a Spanish recipe in Los Placeres de Mi Cocina Judía *by A. Rivka Cohen. The recipe hints of its Turkish Sephardic roots because of its use of bread crumbs. I, in turn, added a little spice typical of that region's cuisine. Serve with any sauce you like or plain with rice.*

1 finely chopped large onion	½ teaspoon cinnamon
¼ cup extra virgin olive oil	¼ teaspoon allspice
3 tablespoons dried bread crumbs	Kosher salt and freshly ground black pepper to taste
3 tablespoons water	3 tablespoons finely chopped toasted pine nuts or almonds
1 large egg	1 pound ground veal (or beef)
2 tablespoons finely chopped parsley	

If making *banderillas* (see step 5):

Red or yellow bell pepper
Cherry tomatoes
Honeydew melon
Olives
Mushrooms

1. Heat a 10-inch frying pan over high heat for 15 seconds. Add the olive oil and heat for another 10 seconds. Add the onion and sauté for 5 minutes or until the onion is soft and lightly golden. Transfer the onions to a 3-quart mixing bowl using a slotted spoon. Leave the oil in the pan.

2. Combine the bread crumbs and water to make a paste. Add to the onions. Add the egg, chopped parsley, cinnamon, allspice, salt, and pepper, and mix thoroughly with a fork.

3. Add the toasted nuts to the bowl along with the meat, and mix with a fork and then your fingertips until all the ingredients are well blended. Shape the meat into balls the size of a walnut.

4. Reheat the pan with the oil from the onion for 15 seconds. Add half of the meatballs or enough to cover the bottom of the pan with room. Cook the meatballs for 10–15 minutes until done, turning often with tongs or a slotted spoon to brown on all sides. Remove the meatballs to a platter, and drain on crumpled paper towel to absorb extra grease. Cook the rest of the meatballs the same way.

5. To serve the meatballs as banderillas tapas (little bites of meatball and vegetables or fruit on toothpicks), place little pieces of sweet red or yellow bell peppers, cherry tomatoes, mushrooms, olives, or small pieces of melon on toothpicks in between two or three

meatballs. You may also serve the meatballs plain over rice or in a pot of sauce of your choice and reheat before serving.

YIELD: 6 SERVINGS

Kitchen Conversations

Discuss your own family's recipes using ground meat. Do the ingredients tell you something about your heritage? Where did your ancestors come from? Were they wealthy or poor? Did they have any connection to Middle Eastern cooks? How could you tell?

TINA'S TIDBITS

- *When cutting or chopping a vegetable, regardless of a person's age, it is easiest to use a chef's knife. This knife is the best choice because you have the most leverage for cutting, the blade is thick enough that there is a distance between the little hands on top and the cutting edge below, and it is the only knife in the repertoire of knives where the blade comes in contact with the cutting board before your hand on the handle. This means that you can rock the knife back and forth to finely mince herbs as well as chop.*
- *Care should be taken with young children at the stove. Older children should be fine turning the meatballs, using a slotted spoon and tongs or a slotted spatula.*

Carnatzlach

My grandma Gussie came from Bucharest, Romania. When the family got together, you could guarantee that patragel (smoked eggplant dip with garlic), potato knishes (the potato was the dough and onions the filling), and carnatzlach would be on the menu.

Carnatzlach or karnatzlack are meatballs that look like little sausages without any casing. (Carnat means "fresh sausage" in Romanian—probably from the Spanish carne, meaning "meat"—and lach at the end of the word is Yiddish for "little.") Grandma didn't grind her own meat the way they probably did in Romania, but her little carnatzlach were delicious!

In 1492, when the Jews were expelled from Spain, the Sultan in Turkey invited them to come live in peace in his large Ottoman Empire. Romania was a part of this empire for over three hundred years. The Sephardim brought their love for ground meat dishes, and the Ottoman use of spices and grilling meats combined over the years to shape the cuisine of Romania.

---

1 tablespoon finely minced garlic
(about 2 large cloves)

1 teaspoon kosher salt or to taste

15 grindings of fresh black pepper or ¼
teaspoon

½ teaspoon ground cumin

½ teaspoon sweet paprika

⅛ teaspoon allspice (optional)

¼ cup club soda

2 tablespoons finely minced fresh
parsley

1 pound ground beef (or ½ pound beef
and ½ pound veal), not too lean

---

1. Mix the garlic, salt, pepper, cumin, paprika, and allspice in a 2-quart glass mixing bowl. Add the club soda to the spices. Set aside for 5 minutes to blend the flavors.

2. Add the parsley and the ground meat to the bowl, and mix together using a fork and a soup spoon. If you feel more comfortable using your hands to mix the ingredients, use your fingertips so the meat won't get tough.

3. Wet your hands with a little water, and then shape the meat into 3 x 1-inch-long logs that are a little pointy on the ends. Do not make them too thin or they will fall apart. Place on a plate.

4. When ready to cook, either grill them outside or on a grill pan on the top of the stove, or broil them in the oven.

5. Using long barbecue tongs and a metal spatula, turn the carnatzlach every 2 minutes or until all sides are browned. They should cook in 7–8 minutes, or less if you like them medium rare.

YIELD: 4-6 SERVINGS

Kitchen Conversations

● What is the difference between club soda and water? Why do you think this recipe calls specifically for club soda?

● How does food from one nearby country affect another? Has Mexican food affected the food choices in Texas, New Mexico, and Arizona? Why? Why not?

TINA'S TIDBITS

• Carnatzlach *often contain large amounts of garlic. This recipe has a lot, but you could add even more if young and old will enjoy it.*
• *When mincing the garlic and the parsley, always use a chef's knife, because it is the safest and most effective way to finely mince food.*

Indian Lamb Meatballs

Many of the Jewish people of India can trace their ancestry back over 2,000 years! Bene Israel Jews are descendants of Kohanim, or high priests, who were shipwrecked on the southwestern coast of India at the time of the Maccabees, and discovered living in the jungles of India in the 1600s. They were far removed from any other Jewish community, but they still said the Sh'ma! Another Jewish sect, the "black" Cochin Jews, claim to have been in India since the time of King Solomon, when their ancestors sailed there looking for spices. The "white" Cochin Jews and the Baghdadi Jews have only been in India for 600 years! They came for the spice trading opportunities and, most likely, to escape the Inquisition in Spain and Portugal.

This recipe uses some of the spices found in India but the use of lamb, cumin, and mint in a meatball speaks volumes about its links to the Jews of the Middle East and Spain. Obviously, matzah meal is a modern touch. Enjoy!

Sauce:

2 tablespoons extra virgin olive oil

1 onion, finely chopped

3 large cloves of garlic, minced

1 teaspoon kosher salt or to taste

20 grindings black pepper
  (½ teaspoon)

28-ounce can recipe-ready fire-roasted
  crushed tomatoes

1 cup chicken broth

1 tablespoon honey

1 teaspoon garam masala

Meatballs:

⅓ cup matzah meal

½ cup loosely packed fresh mint leaves

2 large cloves of garlic

½ teaspoon garam masala

½ teaspoon cumin

¼ teaspoon paprika

¼ teaspoon cinnamon

Pinch of crushed red pepper flakes

1 egg

1 pound ground lamb

2 tablespoons extra virgin olive oil

1 teaspoon lemon juice, as needed

Honey, as needed

1. To make the sauce, heat a 6-quart soup pot over high heat for 15 seconds. Add the oil and heat for another 10 seconds. Add the chopped onion and sauté for 3 minutes until lightly golden.

2. Reduce the heat to medium. Add the minced garlic, salt, and pepper, and sauté for 1 minute until you can smell the garlic but it hasn't yet browned.

3. Add the canned tomatoes, chicken broth, honey, and garam masala. Reduce the heat and simmer, partially covered with a lid, for ½ hour or until you are ready to add the meatballs.

4. To make the meatballs, combine the matzah meal, mint, garlic, and spices in a small food processor work bowl, and pulse the machine on and off until a coarse paste is formed. Use a rubber spatula to scrape the paste into a 4-quart or large mixing bowl.

5. Add the egg to the bowl and mix into the mint mixture with a fork. Add the lamb and gently combine with the other ingredients using a fork or your fingertips. Don't squeeze the meat or the meatballs will be tough. Scoop up a heaping tablespoon of meat and shape

into a 1½-inch meatball. Place on a plate while you make the rest.

6. Heat 2 tablespoons of olive oil for 15 seconds in a 10-inch frying pan or 4-quart pot. Add the meatballs 10 or 12 at a time until the pan is covered but not crowded. Fry the meatballs, turning occasionally with a slotted spoon, until the meatballs are brown. This should take about 10 minutes.

7. As meatballs are done, lift them out of the pot with a slotted spoon and transfer them to the sauce. Quickly finish frying the rest of the meatballs, and place them in the sauce as well.

8. Cook the meatballs in the sauce over low heat. After 15 minutes, add a little lemon juice and more honey, if needed, to give a sweet-and-sour taste.

9. Serve over cooked rice, preferably basmati.

YIELD: 6 SERVINGS

Kitchen Conversations

● Look for India on a map, find Israel, and then trace the ocean route that the Cochin Jews' ancestors traveled with King Solomon.

● Why do you think the tribes who lived in the jungle for thousands of years still recited the *Sh'ma*? Do you think they knew about the Torah or about rabbis? Why or why not?

TINA'S TIDBITS

• *Sautéing onions in a large, deep pot is actually more safe for 6 or 7 year olds because the depth of the vessel prevents splattering from reaching a child's face. However, make sure that you are holding on to the child and/or the pot and that a long handled spoon is used to keep the child's hand away from the rim.*

Polpette Potentina

Many years ago I taught junior high home economics in Mineola, New York. At the end of each semester I would ask students to give a report about one family dish. There was a large Italian community in Mineola, and a student named Carolyn Brienza brought in this recipe. Upon researching the origins of this dish, I learned that Brienza was a town in the Basilicata district in the Potenza province of south, central Italy. Potentina means "from Potenza," and polpette means "meatball." Carolyn probably didn't know the connection of her name to the region and ultimately to the name of the dish.

My excitement came when I found there were many Jewish communities that dated back over two thousand years in this region! Catacombs—underground tunnels often used as burial grounds—were discovered in Venosa containing artifacts and inscriptions in Latin or Greek about Jewish people and with Jewish artifacts drawn on the tomb. One tomb declared the deceased was a twenty-five-year-old Jewish woman brought to Italy from Jerusalem by King Titus to be a slave. Once the Jews were freed, they often remained in that region because it was close to the Mediterranean trade routes. They prospered until the 1600s, when they were temporarily expelled from the region.

Jewish cooks in this region often used fennel in their cooking. Except for the fact that Carolyn's original recipe contained Parmesan cheese, this recipe could have been Jewish. Serve this recipe over pasta with a good-quality, store-bought marinara sauce for a classic Italian dish.

1 cup panko or dried bread crumbs	2 eggs
1 tablespoon minced fresh parsley	¼ cup light red wine
1 teaspoon dried basil	1 pound ground beef
1 teaspoon kosher salt or to taste	3 tablespoons extra virgin olive oil
1 teaspoon fennel seeds, crushed	
15 grindings black pepper (¼ teaspoon)	
¼ teaspoon garlic powder	

1. Place all of the ingredients except the ground beef and the olive oil in a 3-quart mixing bowl. Mix together using a fork or a spatula.

2. Add the meat and mix well to combine all ingredients. Shape the meat into 1-inch balls.

3. Heat a 4-quart pot on high for 20 seconds. Add olive oil and heat for another 15 seconds. Lower the temperature, and then add just enough meatballs so that there is plenty of room between them so they won't stick together. Cook for 15 minutes or until browned on all sides. Remove the meatballs with a slotted spoon and drain on crumpled paper towel. Cook the remaining meatballs in the same way.

4. Return the drained meatballs to the pot, add a quart of your favorite spaghetti sauce, and heat on low until the sauce is hot and the meatballs are done. Serve over spaghetti.

YIELD: 6 SERVINGS

Kitchen Conversations

Did you know that Jews have lived in Italy for thousands of years, Andover five thousand Jewish captives were taken from Jerusalem to be slaves in Rome after the destruction of the Second Temple in 70 CE? Many Jews came to Italy from Spain and Sicily, then a Spanish territory, after 1492. These Jews are Sephardim. However, the Jews whose ancestors lived in Italy since before the fall of the Temple are called Italkim, or "those from Italy."

TINA'S TIDBITS

- *Children two-or three- year old might lose interest after making 2 or 3 meatballs. That is OK. They will know that they helped make the dish and will enjoy pouring the sauce over the meatballs in the pot.*
- *Garlic powder is used in this recipe because it is easier to distribute its flavor throughout the dish than fresh minced garlic.*

Grandma Gladys's Hamburgers

*I*n the summer we imagine hamburgers cooked on the grill. But in many parts of the country when it is cold and snow is on the ground, it isn't possible to cook them outside. This is the way my mother-in-law, who lived on Long Island all of her life, taught me to make hamburgers indoors when I didn't want to fire up the grill outside. These hamburgers always come out plump, juicy, and delicious, and 1 pound of meat can easily make 5 or 6 patties. The secret ingredient is cream of wheat. Unlike bread crumbs and matzah meal, which absorb the juices and dry out the meat, cream of wheat absorbs liquids and expands to make the hamburger juicier. Try it in the pan or on the grill. Either way, I know you will like them.

1–1½ pounds 80% lean ground beef

1 egg

½ teaspoon salt (optional)

Freshly ground black pepper to taste

¼ cup ketchup

¾ teaspoon garlic powder

2 teaspoons Worcestershire sauce

3–4 tablespoons quick-cooking Cream of Wheat

1. Place the ground beef in a 2-quart mixing bowl. Add all of the ingredients on top, and lightly mix the egg and the seasoning together with a fork before thoroughly mixing everything together. You may use a fork or gently combine the meat mixture with your fingertips.

2. Form the meat into five or six 3-inch patties that are 1 inch thick.

3. Heat a dry 10-inch frying pan (with a lid) over high heat for 15 seconds. Carefully place the hamburgers in the hot pan, and lightly press down with a metal spatula so that the bottoms brown quickly.

4. When the hamburgers are brown (but not burnt!) on the bottom and they no longer stick to the pan, turn them over using one or two metal spatulas— whichever is easiest for you.

5. Immediately place the lid tightly over the frying pan and lower the heat to moderately low. Cook for 10–15 minutes, depending on the desired doneness. Serve.

YIELD: 4–5 SERVINGS

Kitchen Conversations

● Reform Judaism has its roots in Germany. Some of the German Jews who emigrated to North America in the 1800s settled in Cincinnati, where they supported the beliefs of Rabbi Isaac Mayer Wise and helped establish Hebrew Union College, where Reform rabbis are now trained. Search the Internet for pictures and history of the school.

TINA'S TIDBITS

• *The most important prerequisite for this recipe is clean hands! Once they have that, children of any age can make the hamburger patties.*
• *The suggested mixing of wet and dry ingredients before you mix them into the meat just prevents streaks of cream of wheat or egg white in the cooked hamburger. Mixing in a separate bowl would just waste ingredients.*

Quick Spiced Turkey Sausage

The first record of sausage making is in Homer's The Odyssey, *written almost three thousand years ago. The word "sausage" is derived from the Latin* salsicia, *meaning something salted. Salt was used to cure meats and preserve them in the days before refrigeration so that they could be stored and eaten later. Sausage making is one of the oldest and most widespread forms of food preservation. In addition to preserving the food with salt, the stuffed intestines (sometimes synthetic tubing is used) filled with bits of meat, butchering leftovers, additional fat, and spices were most often smoked. This not only gave sausages great flavor, but it became one of the best ways to preserve the spirals of pressed meat.*

Since most sausages are made from pork, Jewish cooks had to make their own. Delicatessens were originally owned by Germans who sold pork products. By the 1880s, when Jews started to come to America in larger numbers, Jewish delis were the place to congregate and be able to have kosher meats that resembled the foods from the "old country."

People think sausages are loaded with fat and scraps of meat from who knows where in the animal. However, today there are many leaner forms of sausage made from chicken, turkey, or even vegetables that are nicely flavored and delicious.

The following is an adaptation of a recipe from Judy Zeidler's Master Chefs Cook Kosher *cookbook and TV show.*

½ teaspoon fennel seeds

1 clove fresh garlic

1 pound ground turkey (not white meat only)

¼ teaspoon poultry seasoning (or ground sage)

½ teaspoon dried thyme

½ teaspoon sweet paprika (Hungarian sweet is best)

⅛ teaspoon ground allspice

1 teaspoon black pepper (about 30 grindings)

1 teaspoon kosher salt

2 tablespoons orange or apple liqueur

1 teaspoon honey

1–2 tablespoons water

1 tablespoon vegetable oil

1. Mince the fennel and garlic on a cutting board using a chef's knife.

2. Place ground turkey in a 3-quart glass mixing bowl. Add the spices, liqueur, honey, and 1 tablespoon of the water to the meat, and mix together with your hands, making sure the spices are thoroughly mixed into the turkey.

3. Place the sausage mixture in a pastry bag fitted with a #6 plain tip, or place in a plastic bag, seal, and then cut ¼ inch off one of the corners.

4. Lay a 2-foot sheet of BPA-free plastic wrap on the counter with the long side facing you. Squeeze a line of sausage 3 inches away from the edge down the length of the sheet. Leave 3 inches of space at each end.

5. Roll the plastic wrap neatly over the meat, and then tightly roll up, twisting the ends of the wrap. Tie each end with string or sewing thread, leaving 1 inch of room for air after the end of the meat and before the string.

6. Every 4 inches, twist and tie the sausage with string to make links. Repeat with

other sheets of wrap and the remaining sausage filling until all have been shaped.

7. Put 2 quarts of water in a 3-quart saucepan and heat just to a simmer. Do not let the water boil.

8. Lay the sausages into the barely simmering water and cook for 15 minutes. Using 2 long-handled spatulas or spoons, turn the links over in the water halfway through cooking.

9. Place some ice in a 4-quart bowl and fill halfway with water. Immediately put the sausages in the cold water to cool for a minute. Cut the strings, and remove and discard the plastic wrap. Freeze if not using right away.

10. Heat a 10-inch frying pan or grill pan for 15 seconds. Add 1 tablespoon of vegetable oil, and then heat for another 10 seconds. Sauté the sausages until golden brown on all sides.

11. Serve alone, with breakfast eggs, with sautéed peppers and onions on pasta, or in *Ruota del Faraone* (see page 126).

YIELD: 4-6 SERVINGS

Kitchen Conversations

● Sausages and cured meats like pastrami and corned beef were the staples of the original delis. The oldest delicatessen in America is Katz's Delicatessen in New York City, which was founded in 1888. Did you know that most prominent delicatessens in North America were started by Jewish people? Discuss this association. How did a deli owned by a Jew in a Jewish neighborhood serve the community?

TINA'S TIDBITS

• *This recipe is not difficult, but it should be made with children over the age of nine because it requires good fine motor skills to tie the sausage and eye/hand coordination to pipe and roll the filling.*

• *Artificial sausage casing can be used with a sausage-making attachment on a stand mixer, but the method described in the recipe is more fun and actually easier to make.*

• *The two most important rules for making sausages are to have very clean hands and utensils and to work with very fresh, cold meat.*

This recipe is adapted from Bruce Aidell's recipe in *Master Chefs Cook Kosher* by Judy Zeidler (San Francisco: Chronicle Books, 1998).

WHOLE WHEAT PRETZELS,
PAGE 168

Jewish Bread Basket

Two Pizza Doughs

Here are two recipes for pizza dough, one with a little honey and one made with whole wheat. Both taste great topped with cheese and vegetables, so choose whichever you like. Making your own dough is quick and easy and tastes so much better than the store-bought variety.

Honey Wheat Pizza Dough

3 cups bread flour or all-purpose flour
1 package rapid rise yeast
1 cup water
1 tablespoon honey

2 tablespoons olive oil
1 teaspoon salt
Additional oil to grease bowl

1. Place the flour and yeast in the food processor work bowl. Pulse on and off to combine.

2. Place the remaining ingredients in a 2-cup glass measuring cup and stir to combine. Heat the cup in a microwave oven on high for exactly 1 minute and 15 seconds.

3. Turn the food processor on and immediately add the hot mixture to the work bowl. Process until a ball of dough just begins to form.

4. Knead on a floured surface for 15 strokes. Place in a greased bowl, cover with plastic wrap, and let rise in a warm place until doubled in size (15–20 minutes). You may cover the dough and refrigerate it for up to 3 hours.

5. Punch down the dough, and let it rest for 5 minutes before making pizza.

Whole Wheat Pizza Dough

2¾ cup flour
1¼ cup whole wheat flour
2 packages rapid rise yeast
1¼ cups hot tap water (about 130°F or hot to touch but not enough to burn)

1¼ teaspoon salt
3 tablespoons extra virgin olive oil
Additional oil to grease bowl

1. Place both flours in a food processor workbowl. Pulse on and off 4 times to combine the flours.

2. Stir the yeast into the water and let it sit for a minute until the yeast begins to bubble.

3. Add the yeast mixture, the salt, and the oil to the workbowl. Process until a ball of dough just begins to form.

4. Knead the dough on a lightly floured surface for 1 minute. Lightly grease a bowl with a little additional oil, and then turn the dough in the bowl to coat. Cover the bowl with plastic wrap, and let the dough rise in a warm place for 30 minutes.

5. Punch down the dough. Let the dough rest for 5 minutes before shaping into a pizza crust.

TINA'S TIDBITS

- *Pulsing a food processor on and off is a perfect time to incorporate counting into the cooking activity.*
- *Although the dough should come out of the work bowl easily, **never** let a child put their hands in the workbowl when the blade is in place.*
- *If you don't have an instant-read thermometer to measure the temperature of the water, then just microwave the water for 45–60 seconds to achieve the hot but not scalding temperature needed to grow the yeast.*

Kitchen Conversations

● Touch the dough and try to stretch a little piece of it right after it is mixed in the processor. What does it feel like?

● After the dough rests does it feel different? Why do you think?

● The gluten or protein in the flour needs to rest and relax, or else it tightens and won't stretch well to fit our pizza pans.

Margherita Pizza with Extra Veggies

*F*latbreads have been eaten all over the world for thousands of years. Even the challah brought to the Temple in Jerusalem as an offering each week was a flat bread much like the pita bread we know today.

The first Italian pizzeria, Antica Pizzeria Port'Alba, was founded in 1830 in Naples. It is still selling pizzas to customers today! However, it was another pizzeria in Naples that is responsible for the classic cheese pizza we know today. In 1889, Queen Margherita and King Umberto I visited Naples and went to the Pizzeria Brandi to taste their first pizza. The pizzaioli (pizza maker) at the restaurant was a man by the name of Rafaele Esposito. He created three different flavored pizzas for the king and queen, but the one she loved the best contained the three colors of the Italian flag: red (tomatoes), green (basil), and white (mozzarella cheese). To honor the queen, the pizza was named for her, and restaurants all over the world still list pizza Margherita on their menus.

---

1 recipe pizza dough of your choice
   (see page 160)
2 tablespoons extra virgin olive oil
1 green bell pepper, cut in half and then
   cut into strips
1 red bell pepper, cut in half and then
   cut into strips
8 ounces mozzarella cheese, grated

8 ounces fontina cheese, grated
26-ounce jar of pizza sauce or marinara
   sauce
16 basil leaves, torn into pieces
½ cup diced mushrooms
½ red onion, sliced into thin half rings
Extra olive oil for greasing pans

---

1. Make the pizza dough of your choice, and divide into 2 pieces.

2. Heat 2 tablespoons of oil in a 10-inch frying pan for 10 seconds. Add the bell peppers and sauté until soft, about 5 minutes. Set aside.

3. Combine the grated cheeses in a 2-quart mixing bowl and set aside.

4. Heat the oven to 475°F. Lightly grease two 12-inch pizza pans or two cookie sheets with a little extra olive oil. Set aside.

5. Using a rolling pin, roll out each piece of dough to make a 9-inch round. Make sure that the center of the dough is thinner than the edges.

6. By hand, stretch each piece of dough from the center outward to make a round that is at least 1 inch larger than your pan or around 12 inches if you are using a cookie sheet. Place on the oiled pans.

7. Spread ½–1 cup of sauce on each round of dough. Do not use too much sauce or your pizza will be soggy. Scatter the basil over the sauce, and then top with the cheese mixture. Top each pizza with some of the sautéed peppers and the remaining ingredients.

8. Bake about 15 minutes or until the cheese is melted and the crust is golden. Let the pizza rest for 5 minutes before cutting.

YIELD: 6-8 SERVINGS

- *Children love to decorate their own pizzas. Why not have an assortment of seasonal vegetables arranged in small dishes so that they can pick and choose which vegetables to place on their pizza?*
- *Young children should not sauté the peppers, since the water content in the pepper will make the oil spatter.*
- *A five-year-old could help put the cold pizza pan in the oven (especially if you are putting the pan on a big wooden pizza peel first). However, an adult needs to remove the hot pizza, because the oven is set on a very high temperature and the oil used to grease the pan could drip and burn a child.*

Kitchen Conversations

● Did you know soldiers were responsible for the popularity of pizza in Italy and in North America? Although Italians were eating flat pieces of bread—focaccia—for centuries, it is part of Italian mythology that the Roman soldiers stationed in Jerusalem grew to like the Jewish flatbread, which was probably matzah, and when they returned to Italy after the destruction of the Second Temple, they brought their love of the bread with them along with the Jewish slaves.

● Have you ever gone on vacation, tried a new food while you were away, and wanted to eat it often when you came home? What food was it? Can you make it or buy it in your town?

Bagels

Bagels, the boiled and baked dough with the round shape, have been mainstays in the Jewish kitchen for hundreds of years. Whether it is the round roll with the hole that was eaten in Eastern Europe or the hard round ka'ak biscuit eaten in the Middle East, circular bread has always represented prosperity and the circle of life. Many Jews in Eastern Europe were so superstitious that they wore bagels on a string around their necks to fight off any evil spirits around them. A bagel peddler could easily sell his chewy rolls, piled high on a stick, to customers on the street or to workers in the field, so the bagel was made into a ring. (In German, bagel means "ring" or "bracelet.") When Jewish immigrants came to North America in the 1800s, they brought the love and lore of bagels with them, and many bagel stores opened in New York. After World War II, bagels with all their mystical powers of protection and prosperity were served with expensive smoked fish to ensure that the person eating would appear prosperous. The tradition of bagels with cream cheese and lox was born.

4 –4½ cups bread flour	3 tablespoons sugar
2 packages rapid rise yeast	1 tablespoon salt
1½ cups water	1 tablespoon sugar for boiling bagels

1. Place 2 cups of the flour and the yeast in a 4-quart mixing bowl. Using a handheld electric mixer, mix for 5 seconds on low to combine. Set aside.

2. Measure the water in a liquid measuring cup and add 3 tablespoons of sugar and the salt. Stir with a spoon to combine, and then microwave on high for 45 seconds or until the water is 125°F.

3. Stir the liquid again with a spoon to combine and immediately pour into the bowl with the flour. Mix on low speed for ½ minute. Remove the mixer from bowl, and scrape down the sides of the bowl with a rubber spatula. Resume beating the mixture on medium for 3 minutes. Unplug the mixer and remove the beaters. Scrape the beaters clean.

4. By hand, stir in enough of the remaining flour (about 2 cups) to make a stiff dough. Use some of the extra flour to lightly flour your counter or a pastry board, and knead the dough until it is smooth and elastic (about 5–7 minutes). Place the mixing bowl over the dough on the counter, and let the dough rest for 15 minutes.

5. Using a chef's knife, cut the dough in half and then each half into 6–8 pieces (depending on the size bagel desired).

6. Shape each piece into a ball. Flatten the ball to about ½ inch. Flour your finger and poke a hole through the center of the ball. Stretch the hole gently to make it bigger, and adjust the shape to make it round. Lightly cover the finished bagels with a clean dish towel or plastic wrap, and let rise for 20 minutes.

7. Preheat the oven to 375°F. Fill a 6-quart pot with 4 quarts of water and the remaining 1 tablespoon of sugar. Bring the water to a boil. Reduce the heat to a simmer.

8. Place 3–4 bagels in the water top side down, and cook for 3 minutes. Using 1 or 2 slotted spatulas or spoons, turn

the bagels over, and cook 3 minutes more. Remove the bagels with a slotted spatula to drain, and place on a greased cookie sheet or cookie sheet lined with parchment paper.

9. Bake the boiled bagels for 25–30 minutes or until golden brown and baked through.

TINA'S TIDBITS

If you are working with young children, you will find this recipe is easier to make in a stand electric mixer, using a paddle first for mixing and then the dough hook for the kneading. This eliminates the safety and coordination issues of very young children as well as the time necessary to knead the dough by hand. Attention spans are short and kneading for 5 or more minutes will lose the cook under the age of six.

It is very important to remember to unplug a handheld mixer before you remove the beaters. Little hands can accidently push the on/off button and get fingers caught in the beaters if the machine is plugged in.

Kitchen Conversations

● Would you wear a bagel around your neck? Do you or anyone you know wear other symbols for good luck? Examples include the blue evil eye from Turkey and the Middle East, or the *hamsa* (or "hand") from Israel. Do you think these charms really work? Why or why not?

● Ancient cultures in Egypt and China had round pastries. Explore the Internet to see if you can find examples of these. How are they similar to bagels?

Garlic and Herb Monkey Bread

Monkey bread is a variation on the sweet, cinnamon-laced, buttery yeast cakes originally popular in the Middle East that became equally popular in Europe once spices were introduced to European kitchens. The German kuchen is a good example of this rich yeast cake. No food historian knows for sure how it got its name, but one suggestion is that the finished cake looks a lot like a bunch of monkeys piled on top of each other.

By the mid 1900's monkey bread became popular in American kitchens because it was easy to make (especially if the cook used store-bought biscuit dough), was rich in flavor because each ball of dough was rolled in butter and then spices, and was elegantly shaped in a tall crown. Later, the cake was also made savory with herbs and cheese.

The shape of the cake is due to the Bundt pan, and the Bundt pan is a direct result of a request by two Jewish women belonging to the Minneapolis chapter of Hadassah. In 1950, these women asked the owners of Nordic Ware to produce a kuglehof pan, similar to the porcelain one the chapter's president had received from her grandmother in Germany. The company made a few aluminum versions for the Hadassah members and sold a limited number to a local department store. Originally the company named the pan Bund because bund, in German, means a gathering or party. When Nordic Ware trademarked the name of the pan they renamed it Bundt and the pan's popularity is now culinary history.

3¾ cup bread flour

1 package rapid rise yeast

1 teaspoon salt

1¼ cup milk (add 1 tablespoon butter if using skim milk)

¼ cup sugar

1 egg

¼ cup extra virgin olive oil

½ stick unsalted butter

2 tablespoons extra virgin olive oil

1 teaspoon minced fresh oregano (or ½ teaspoon dried)

1 teaspoon minced fresh rosemary (or ½ teaspoon dried)

2 teaspoons freshly minced basil (or 1 teaspoon dried)

3 large cloves of garlic, finely minced

Pinch of kosher salt

5 grindings of black pepper

¼ cup finely grated Parmesan cheese

---

1. Place 3½ cups of the flour, the yeast, and the salt in the bowl of an electric mixer, fitted with a dough hook, and combine for 5 seconds on low speed.

2. Measure the milk into a 2-cup glass measuring cup, and add the sugar. Place in a microwave and heat on high for 1 minute and 20 seconds.

3. With the mixer running on low, stir the milk mixture once and then add to the flour. Immediately add the egg and then the oil. Knead by machine for seven minutes until the dough is soft but not sticky. Add a little more flour if the dough seems too moist.

4. Remove the dough to a lightly floured counter, and knead 5 or 6 times. Grease a 2-quart bowl with a little oil, and add the dough, turning once to coat lightly. Cover with plastic wrap and place in a warm or draft-free area. Let rise for 45 minutes or until the dough doubles in size.

5. While the dough is rising, mix the butter, oil, herbs, salt, and pepper in a 1½-quart glass bowl, and microwave until the butter is melted, about 1 minute.

6. Lightly oil a Bundt pan. Divide the dough into fourths using a chef's knife, and then cut each section into 12–16 pieces. Shape each piece into a ball. Dip each ball into the garlic herb butter, and place facedown in the pan. Sprinkle the finished row with some of the Parmesan cheese.

7. Continue with the remaining dough, creating rows of balls, filling in the gaps, and sprinkling each layer with some more of the Parmesan cheese.

8. Let the dough rise in the pan for 20–25 minutes. Preheat the oven to 350°F. Bake for 30–35 minutes until the bread has risen and turned golden. Cool for 5 minutes, and then invert onto a plate and serve. Pull on the bread and portions will easily come apart.

YIELD: 10 OR MORE SERVINGS

Kitchen Conversations

Discuss the story of the invention of the Bundt pan. Any cake pan could have been used to make the Hadassah president's grandmother's recipe, but she felt she needed the same shape to achieve the desired cake texture. What did the pan also mean to her and other grandchildren of German ancestors?

TINA'S TIDBITS

- *Making bread in a mixer with a dough hook is very easy to do, but remember not to leave a child unattended while the mixer is plugged in. A simple brush of the hand can turn the mixer on.*
- *Since this dough does not require a long time to rise, cleaning the kitchen and making the butter/herb dip will probably take up the time it takes to let the dough rise.*
- *If a child is very young, store-bought bread dough or prepared biscuit dough can be used to save some time and still have fun.*
- *To make this cake sweet instead of savory, eliminate the garlic, herbs, and cheese, use an additional 2 tablespoons of butter instead of the olive oil, and add 1 tablespoon of sugar and ½ teaspoon ground cinnamon to the butter, and proceed to layer the balls of dough.*

Whole Wheat Pretzels

I f bagels represented good luck, prosperity, and an inexpensive way to feed the hungry and poor in European Jewish communities, the pretzel served the same purpose in the Christian community. Invented by a sixth-century monk, leftover bread dough was twisted to look like arms crossed over a chest in prayer. Soon the pretzels were used to reward students and were included in marriage ceremonies to represent two halves united in marriage. Another story has pretzel bakers in sixteenth-century Vienna baking pretzels at night and hearing the attacking Ottoman soldiers tunneling under the thick city walls. The Austrian army was notified, and the city was saved. Pretzels were later popularized as an inexpensive food to feed the poor.

2 cups whole wheat flour
2 cups all-purpose flour
1 package yeast (rapid rise or regular dried yeast)
1⅓ cups water

3 tablespoons vegetable oil
1 tablespoon honey
1 teaspoon salt
Kosher salt (optional)

Orange Glaze (optional):

¼ teaspoon orange extract
1 cup confectioners' sugar
2–3 tablespoons milk or water

1. Stir the two flours together in a 1-quart bowl.

2. Combine 1½ cups of the flour mixture and the yeast in a 3-quart bowl.

3. Combine the water, oil, honey, and salt in a 2-cup glass measuring cup, and microwave for 45 seconds or until it is hot to the touch but not scalding.

4. Stir the hot liquid mixture with a spatula to combine, and add to the bowl with the flour and yeast. Beat with a wooden spoon for 2 minutes.

5. Add 2 cups of the flour mixture to the bowl to make a firm dough. If the dough is still very soft and sticky, add more flour ¼ cup at a time.

6. Knead by hand for 3–5 minutes on a lightly floured counter (use some of the remaining flour until the dough is smooth). Let rest for 10 minutes on the counter, covered by the turned-over used mixing bowl.

7. Cut the dough into 12 pieces, and roll each into a 15-inch rope. Shape the ropes into pretzels, bringing each end of the rope toward you and crossing the ends in the middle to create a pretzel shape.

8. For salt pretzels: Brush each pretzel with a little water and then press the top of the pretzel in a dish of kosher salt.

9. Place the pretzels on a cookie sheet lined with parchment paper or a lightly greased cookie sheet.

10. Bake at 425°F for 15–20 minutes until golden.

11. For glazed pretzels: Whisk the orange extract, sugar, and milk or water with a small bar whisk in a 1-quart bowl until smooth. Either brush the glaze on the warm pretzels or dip the tops of the pretzels into a dish of the glaze. Allow the glaze to harden for a few minutes before serving.

YIELD: 12 LARGE PRETZELS

Kitchen Conversations

Just like pretzels were used in the Christian community to teach and tell stories, many Jewish foods are both tasty and symbolic, like round challot for Rosh HaShanah or hamantaschen for Purim. Can you think of other examples? How could you reshape the pretzel dough in this recipe to tell a Jewish story?

TINA'S TIDBITS

- *Do not allow small children to retrieve the hot sugar water from the microwave. Children can pour in the liquid, but a young child is generally not tall enough to safely remove the hot liquid.*
- *Let children create their own style of twists or shapes.*
- *Baked pretzels may also be dipped in melted butter and then in cinnamon and sugar.*

Appendix 1: Recipes by Course

Appetizers

- Beet Hummus
- Hungarian Cabbage Strudel
- *Kyeftes de Karne Kon Muezas* (Meatballs with Nuts)
- *Mast o Khiar* (Persian Cucumber Yogurt Salad)
- Quesadillas
- Syrian *Charoset*

Soups and Salads

- Barley Salad with Fresh Herbs and Pomegranate
- Basic Chicken Soup
- Classic Jewish Deli Chicken Salad
- Chicken-Filled Kreplach
- Ethiopian Peanut Soup
- Kale, Mango, and Almond Salad with Honey Ginger Dressing
- Krupnick (Vegetarian Mushroom Barley Soup)
- Meggy Leves (Hungarian Cherry Soup)
- Nancy's Fresh Corn Salad
- Quick and Easy Tomato Vegetable Soup

Main Dishes

- Breaded Chicken Schnitzel
- Carnatzlach
- Challah Cheese Soufflé
- Challah French Toast
- Chicken Salad Veronique with Avocados
- Grandma Gladys's Hamburgers
- Grandma Lucille's Blintz Soufflé
- Indian Lamb Meatballs
- *Kyeftes de Karne Kon Muezas* (Meatballs with Nuts)
- Manicotti with Tomato Sauce
- Matzah Brie
- Passover *Migas*
- Polpette Potentina
- Potato-Crusted Fish
- Quick Spiced Turkey Sausage
- Roasted Chicken South African Style
- *Ruota del Faraone* (Pharaoh's Wheels)
- Supermarket Checkout Chicken
- Three-Ingredient Brisket

Side Dishes

- Applesauce
- Bread Kugel with Dried Fruit and Sun-Dried Tomatoes
- Corn Pudding
- Pareve Apple Raisin Kugel
- Pareve Apricot Orange Noodle Kugel
- Persian Cauliflower and Raisin *Kuku*
- Persian Kuku with Spinach, Pine Nuts, and Raisins
- Potato Onion Kugel
- Roasted Butternut Squash with Apples and Onions
- Sweet Potato and Carrot Latkes
- Zella's Classic Noodle Kugel

Breads

- Bagels
- Basic Easy Challah
- Garlic and Herb Monkey Bread
- Margherita Pizza with Extra Veggies
- Round Algerian Challah
- Two Pizza Doughs
- Whole Wheat Pretzels

Desserts

- Almond Poppy Seed Pound Cake
- Challah "Babka" Bread Pudding
- Chocolate Chip Mystery Mandlebrot
- Chocolate Filling for Hamentaschen (Gluten-Free)
- Classic New York Egg Cream
- Delicious and Easy Rice Kugel
- Double Coconut Chocolate Macaroons
- *GeshmirtaMatzah*
- Gluten-Free Hamantaschen Dough (Dairy)
- Green Tea–Jasmine Sorbet with Assorted Fruits
- Passover Granola
- Quick Honey Cake
- Zimsterne Cookies

Appendix 2: Recipes by Kashrut Components

Dairy

- Almond Poppy Seed Pound Cake
- Challah "Babka" Bread Pudding*
- Challah Cheese Soufflé
- Challah French Toast*
- Chocolate Filling for Hamantaschen (Gluten-Free)
- Classic New York Egg Cream
- Corn Pudding*
- Delicious and Easy Rice Kugel
- Garlic and Herb Monkey Bread*
- *Geshmirta Matzah*
- Gluten-Free Hamentaschen Dough
- Grandma Lucille's Blintz Soufflé
- Hungarian Cabbage Strudel*
- Manicotti with Tomato Sauce
- Margherita Pizza with Extra Veggies
- *Mast o Khiar* (Persian Cucumber Yogurt Salad)
- Matzah Brie
- MeggyLeves (Hungarian Cherry Soup)
- Passover Granola
- Passover Migas
- Potato-Crusted Fish*
- Quesadillas
- Quick Honey Cake
- Zella's Classic Noodle Kugel
- Zimsterne Cookies*

Meat

- Basic Chicken Soup
- Bread Kugel with Dried Fruit and Sun-Dried Tomatoes*
- Breaded Chicken Schnitzel
- Brisket, Three-Ingredient
- Carnatzlach
- Chicken Salad Veronique with Avocado
- Chicken-Filled Kreplach
- Classic Jewish Deli Chicken Salad
- Ethiopian Peanut Soup
- Grandma Gladys's Hamburgers
- Indian Lamb Meatballs
- *Kyeftes de Karne kon Muezes* (Meatballs with Nuts)
- Polpette Potentina
- Potato Onion Kugel*
- Quick Spiced Turkey Sausage
- Roasted Chicken South African Style
- *Ruota del Faraone* (Pharaoh's Wheels)
- Super market Checkout Chicken

Pareve

- Applesauce
- Bagels
- Barley Salad with Fresh Herbs and Pomegranate
- Basic Easy Challah
- Beet Hummus
- Chocolate Chip Mystery Mandlebrot
- Double Coconut Chocolate Macaroons
- Green Tea–Jasmine Sorbet with Assorted Fruits
- Kale, Mango, and Almond Salad
- Krupnick (Vegetarian Mushroom Barley Soup)
- Nancy's Fresh Corn Salad
- Pareve Apple Raisin Kugel
- Pareve Apricot Orange Noodle Kugel
- Persian Cauliflower and Raisin Kuku
- Persian Kuku with Spinach, Pine Nuts, and Raisins
- Quick and Easy Tomato Vegetable Soup
- Roasted Butternut Squash with Apples and Onions
- Round Algerian Challah
- Sweet Potato and Carrot Latkes
- Syrian Charoset
- Two Pizza Doughs
- Whole Wheat Pretzels

*This recipe can easily be made pareve by substituting pareve ingredients for dairy or meat ingredients.

Bibliography

Anavi, Yvette. *Sephardic Cuisine*. Fremont, CA: Beyond Borders Publishing, 2005.

Batmanglii, Najmieh. *Food of Life: Ancient Persian and Modern Iranian Cooking and Ceremonies*. Washington, DC: Mage Publishing, 2011.

Blech, Benjamin. *Eyewitness to Jewish History*. Hoboken, NJ: John Wiley & Sons, 2004.

Bonanome, A., Kawaji, T., Levine, B., Pagnan, A., Schwartz, R., and Stanton, R. *Mediterranean Cooking with Olive Oil*. Madrid: International Olive Oil Council, 1996.

Bremzen, Anya. *The Greatest Dishes!* New York: HarperCollins, 2004.

Caldicott, Chris, and Carolyn Caldicott. *The Spice Routes*. San Francisco: Soma Books, 2001.

Clabrough, Chantal. *A Pied Noir Cookbook*. New York: Hippocrene Books, 2005.

Claiborne, Craig. *International Cook Book*. New York: Harper & Row, 1971.

Cohen, A. Rivka. *Los Placeres de Mi Cocina Judía*. Barcelona: Parsifal Ediciones, 2003.

Corriher, Shirley. *CookWise: The Hows and Whys of Successful Cooking*. New York: William Morrow, 1997.

Dweck, Poopa. *Aromas of Aleppo: The Legendary Cuisine of Syrian Jews*. New York: Harper Collins Publisher, 2007

Gilbert, Martin. *Jewish History Atlas*. New York: Macmillan, 1969.

Gitlitz, David, and Linda Davidson. *A Drizzle of Honey*. New York: St. Martin's Griffin, 1999.

Goldman, Rivka. *Mama Nazima's Jewish-Iraqi Cuisine*. New York: Hippocrene Books, 2006.

Goodman, Hanna. *Jewish Cooking around the World*. New York: Jewish Publication Society of America, 1969.

Goodman, N., Marcus, R., and Woolhandler, S. *The Good Book Cookbook: Recipes from Biblical Times*. New York: Dodd, Mead 1986.

Grossman, Ruth, and Bob Grossman. *The Italian-Kosher Cookbook*. New York: Paul S. Eriksson, 1964.

Herbst, Sharon. *Food Lover's Companion*. 3rd ed. New York: Barron's Educational Series, 2001.

Hyman, Mark. "How Eating at Home Can Save Your Life." *Huffington Post*, January 9, 2011. http://www.huffingtonpost.com/dr-mark-hyman/family-dinner-how_b_806114.html.

International Olive Oil Council, comp. *Cooking with Olives*. Madrid: International Olive Oil Council, n.d.

International Olive Oil Council, comp. *Mediterranean Cooking with Olive Oil*. Madrid: International Olive Oil Council, 1996.

Levi, Zion, and Hani Agabria. *The Yemenite Cook Book*. New York: Seaver Books, 1988.

Liebman, Malvina W. *Jewish Cookery from Boston to Baghdad*. Cold Spring, NY: Nighin-Gale Resources, 1975.

Lopez, Ruth. *Chocolate: The Nature of Indulgence*. New York: Harry Abrams, 2002.

Machlin, Edda. *Classic Italian Jewish Cooking*. New York: HarperCollin, 2005.

Marks, Gil. *Encyclopedia of Jewish Food*. Hoboken, NJ: John Wiley & Sons, 2010.

Marks, Gil. *The World of Jewish Cooking*. New York: Simon & Schuster, 1996.

Nathan, Joan. *The Foods of Israel Today*. New York: Alfred Knopf, 2001.

Poses, Steven, Anne Clark, and Becky Roller. *The Frog Commissary Cook Book*. Garden City, NY: Doubleday, 1985.

Roden, Claudia. *Arabesque: A Taste of Morocco, Turkey, & Lebanon*. New York: Alfred Knopf, 2008.

Roden, Claudia. *The Book of Jewish Food*. New York: Random House, 1996.Rose, Evelyn.

The New Complete International Jewish Cookbook. New York: Galahad Books,1992.

Shaul, Moshe, Aldina Quintana Rodriguez, and Zelda Ovadia, eds. *El Gizado Sefaradi*. Zaragosa, Spain: Ibercaja, 1995.

Shosteck, Patti. *A Lexicon of Jewish Cooking*. Chicago: Contemporary Books Inc., 1979.

The Silver Spoon. New York: Phaidon Press, 2005.

Sisterhood Board of Mikve Israel-Emanuel. *Recipes from the Jewish Kitchens of Curacao*. Curacao: DrukkerijScherpenheuvel N.V., 1982.

Strassfeld, Michael, *The Jewish Holidays*, New York, Harper Collins, 1985

Twena, Pamela. *The Sephardic Table*. New York: Houghton Mifflin, 1998.

Union of Jewish Women, comp. *Union Jubilee Cook Book*. Cape Town, 1982.

WIZO Panama. *El Sabor de la Tradición*. Panama: WIZO Panama, 1993.

Wright, Clifford. *A Mediterranean Feast*. New York: William Morrow, 1999.

Zeidler, Judy, *Master Chefs Cook Kosher*, San Francisco,Chronicle Books, 1998

Index